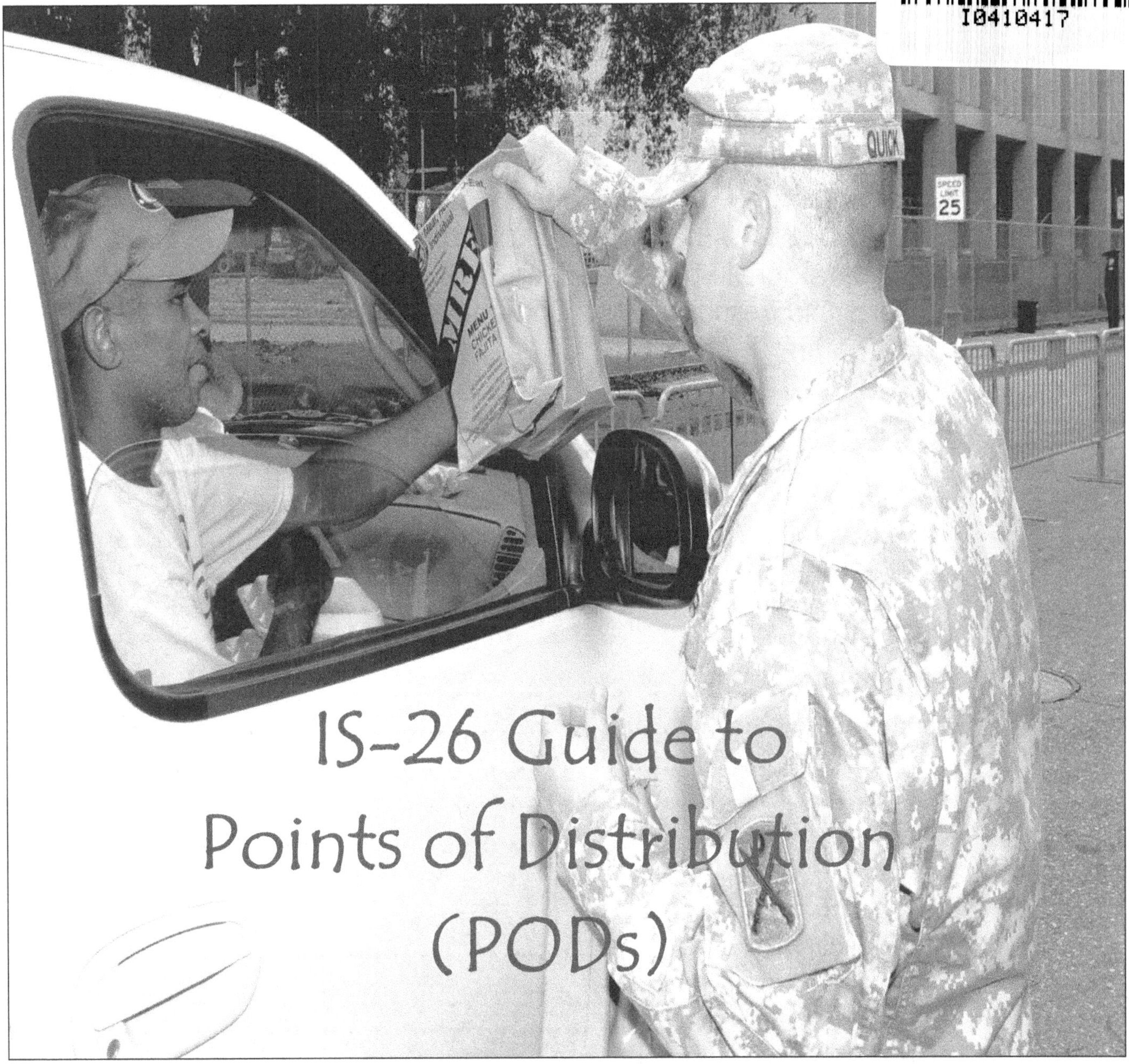

IS-26 Guide to
Points of Distribution
(PODs)

December 2008

Table of Contents

Objectives

By the end of this Guide you will be able to:

- Describe Points of Distribution

- Explain how Points of Distribution are set up and operated

- Understand how to supervise a Point of Distribution Staff

Lesson 1

INTRODUCTION

Lesson Objectives

By the end of this lesson you will be able to:

- Describe Points of Distribution

- Delineate the common forms of commodity distribution

What are Points of Distribution or PODs?

Points of Distribution

- Points of Distribution are centralized locations where the public picks up life sustaining commodities following a disaster or emergency

- Commodities usually include shelf stable food and water

During a disaster, one method of issuing supplies may not be enough. A Local Emergency Management Agency (LEMA) could use other distribution systems or use all of them at once. All three complement each other and provide expanded distribution coverage.

Mobile delivery is a method that utilizes vehicles to drive into an affected area and provide commodities at different drop locations or where the need is identified. This type of distribution is common in rural areas and where roads are damaged.

Direct delivery is coordinating with a specific location, such as a shelter, feeding site, or hospital for the delivery of specific items and quantities. These commodities could be food, water, comfort kits etc. Direct deliveries are usually larger in size and more specific in commodity type than what is delivered through mobile delivery.

Points of Distribution are centralized points where supplies are delivered and the public travels to the site to pick up the commodities.

For this Guide, we will focus on Points of Distribution or PODs.

PODs can accommodate vehicle traffic (drive-thru), pedestrian traffic (walk thru), and mass transit traffic (bus or rail).

Each person or vehicle receives a set amount of supplies. The recommended amount is for each person/vehicle to receive enough for a household of three. The amount of supplies provided will differ depending on the type of transportation used. For instance, more supplies are provided to someone in a car than to a pedestrian who must hand carry items.

Commodities provided can include, but are not limited to, shelf stable food, bottled water, and limited amounts of ice, tarps, and blankets. Local Emergency Management Agency (LEMA) will determine the actual commodities and set quantity of each.

Summary

In this lesson you learned how to:

- Describe Points of Distribution

- Delineate the common forms of commodity distribution

STAFFING

Lesson Objectives

By the end of this lesson you will be able to:

- Describe the organizational structure of a Point of Distribution

- Understand the Local Emergency Management Agency (LEMA) is the primary authority for the activation, operation, and demobilization of the PODs.

- Identify the roles and responsibilities of:
  - Local Emergency Management Agencies (LEMAs)
  - POD staff

Organizational Structure

The Local Emergency Management Agency is the primary authority for the activation, operation, and demobilization of the PODs.

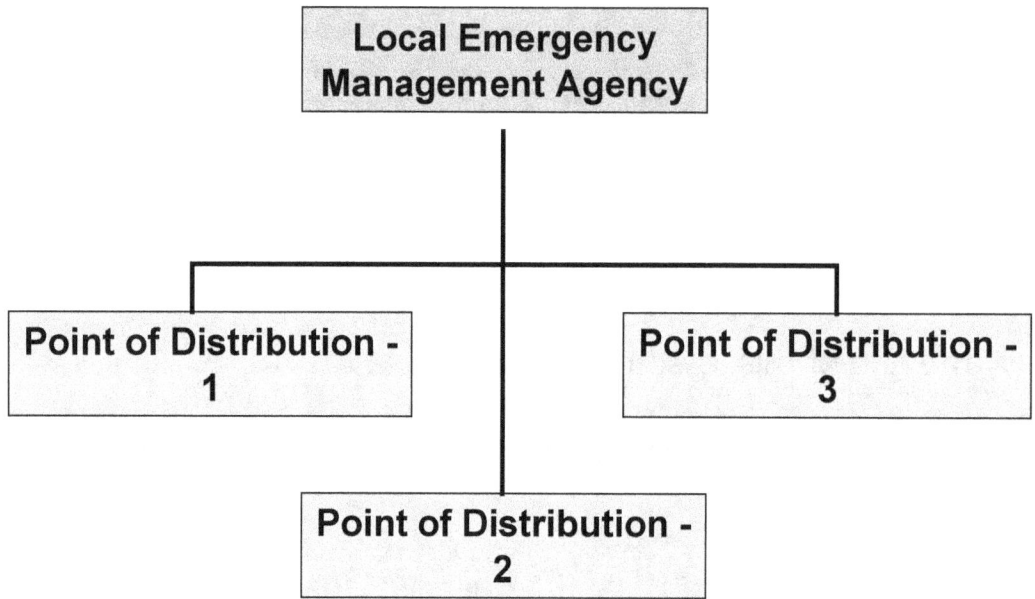

The determination to activate, operate, and demobilize a POD is at the discretion of the Local Emergency Management Agency (LEMA).

LEMA *determines* the location and type of POD based on:

- needs analysis
- population density, and
- current methods of commodity distribution

LEMA *coordinates* the activation of PODs based on:

- public need
- types of resources needed
- infrastructure capability, and
- availability of resources

LEMA *designates* resources for each POD

- type of distributed commodity
- amount of distributed commodity
- POD material handling equipment

LEMA *activates* a POD. It is important not to activate without guidance from LEMA because:

- Workers may not be covered for workers compensation or liability
- LEMA may not have the resources to supply the POD
- LEMA may not have the capability to communicate or access the POD
- LEMA may decide not to utilize PODs as a form of public commodity distribution
- This may cause false expectations or false hope from surrounding citizens and residents

LEMA is responsible for:

Providing POD Manager Training

Selecting POD staff and locations
- Ensuring that POD locations support the population density, needs, and takes into account other forms of public commodity distribution

Registering POD workers
- At a minimum, POD Managers should be registered as an Emergency Worker in accordance with local laws.
- It is suggested that all POD primary staff are registered

Activating PODs
- Determining the need and availability of PODs for activation

Supplying PODs
- Providing appropriate allocations of commodities for distribution based on population densities and expected public need
- Providing material handling equipment and staff support resources

Demobilizing PODs
- Determining when to demobilize PODs based on need and infrastructure restoration
- Coordinating the receipt of excess resources
- Coordinating the removal of material handling equipment and staff support resources
- Restoring sites to original specifications
- Collecting and processing all paperwork associated with the POD

Conducting POD Reset
- Coordinating the replenishment of POD Kits
- Conducting After Action Reviews
- Recognizing participating organizations for service to their community

This is the management structure of a POD. Under the direction of the POD manager, the POD operates using two teams:

- Loading Team
- Support Team

POD Staff

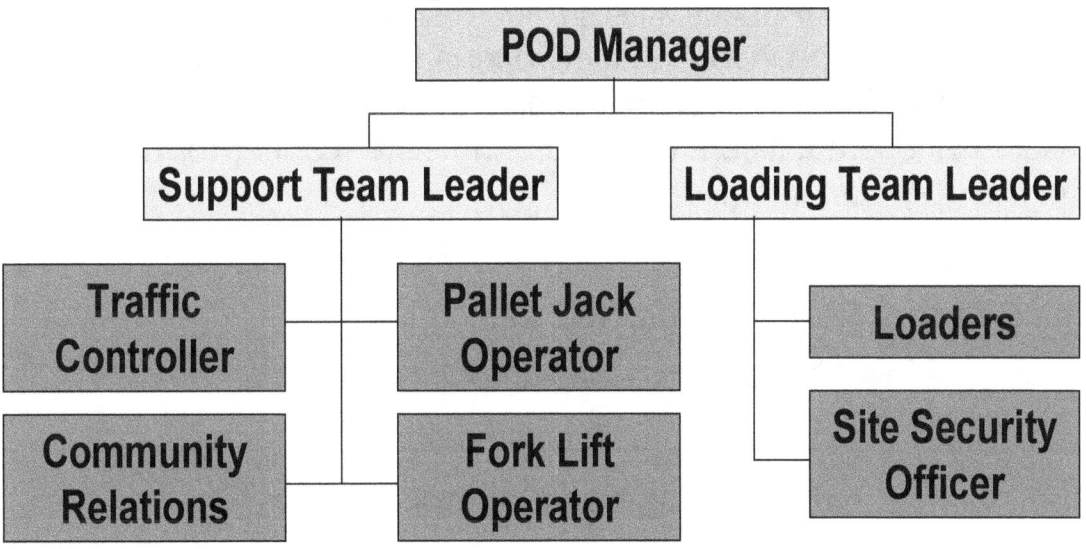

The POD Manager has overall responsibility for the safe operation of the POD. This includes all staff and resources on site throughout the activation. The POD Manager reports to LEMA for guidance and information. The POD Manager is also the primary safety officer and ensures all operations are conducted in a safe manner for the staff and the POD customers.

The Support Team *supports* the loading line by:

- Resupplying loading points
- Unloading bulk commodities
- Maintaining traffic control
- Providing community relations

The Support team *consists* of:

- Support Team Leader
- Traffic Control
- Community Relations
- Fork Lift Operator
- Pallet Jack Operator

The Support Team Leader *supervises* all support operations including:

- Ensuring equipment used on site has been inspected, maintained, and used in a safe manner
- Coordinating supply truck movement on site
- Conducting resupply operations including downloading commodities and resupplying the loading line
- Maintaining accountability of all commodities received, on hand, and distributed from the site
- Maintaining all paperwork relating to resource accountability and providing daily resource reports to LEMA

The Traffic Controller *manages* the movement of vehicles through the POD; not just customer vehicles but also tractor trailers. The Traffic Controller directly controls the movement of vehicles in the vehicle lane and oversees the safety of loaders on the vehicle line.

All issues with customer vehicles, such as breakdowns, are coordinated with and directed by the Traffic Controller or Support Team Leader.

The Community Relations staff *serves* as the central point of contact for media and public relations on the site.

The Community Relations staff *works* with LEMA's Public Information Officer (PIO) to distribute public information (flyers, handouts etc.)

The Fork Lift Operator *manages* the movement of pallets to and from the resupply vehicle(s). This includes resupplying the loading line.

Fork Lift Operators MUST BE QUALIFIED TO OPERATE THE EQUIPMENT!

The Pallet Jack Operator is responsible for the movement of pallets to and from the loading line and removing empty pallets.

Pallet Jack Operators MUST BE FAMILIAR WITH THE EQUIPMENT!

The Loading Team *conducts* loading operations and sustainment of staff. The support team supports the loading line by:

- Conducting customer commodity loading
- Sustaining staff operations including:
    - Restrooms
    - Break Areas
    - Trash Removal
    - Staff Feeding
    - Establishing Shift Schedules

The Loading Team *consists* of:

- Loading Team Leader
- Loaders
- Site Security Officer

The Loading Team Leader *supervises* all loading and sustainment operations including:

- Loading of supplies into customer vehicles
- Ensuring the Loading Line has adequate supplies
- Coordinating the staff sustainment and care including:
    - Restrooms
    - Rest Areas
    - Feeding
    - Shift Schedules
- Oversees site security and coordinates with local law enforcement for assistance

Loaders *are responsible* for loading set quantities of supplies into customer vehicles. Loaders also coordinate with the Support Team for resupply of the loading line.

The Site Security Officer *is responsible* for securing the POD site and ensuring/maintaining good order.

The Site Security Officer will be the primary staff member that will work with angered or agitated customers. The Site Security Officer should be a law enforcement officer or an individual trained in security operations.

Summary

In this lesson you learned about:

- The organization structure of a POD

- The primary authority for the activation, operation, and demobilization of the PODs.

- Roles and responsibilities of LEMA and the POD staff

Lesson 3

SETUP

Lesson Objectives

By the end of this lesson you will be able to discuss:

- How to develop your site layout

- How to activate a POD

- How to support a POD site and staff

Developing your site Layout

When developing your site layout, there are several considerations to keep in mind:

- What type of POD? Vehicle, pedestrian or mass transit? There are different set up requirements for each.

- Are there entrance and exit concerns? Is there more than one entry/exit point?

- What is the traffic flow around the site? Will residents have to cross a busy street? Will having a POD at this location halt the surrounding traffic and cause a traffic jam? Will this site impede emergency response vehicles?

- Are there turns within the site or at the entry/exit points that require extra maneuvering? Can large semi trucks get in and out without assistance?

- Prior to setting up and activating a POD, make sure there are no hazards threatening the site or staff. Is the POD in a location that may flood? Is there debris on the site that could injure someone? Consider new hazards the disaster has created. Is there a structure that could fall on the POD? Is there a fire burning nearby that could affect the site?

Site Layout

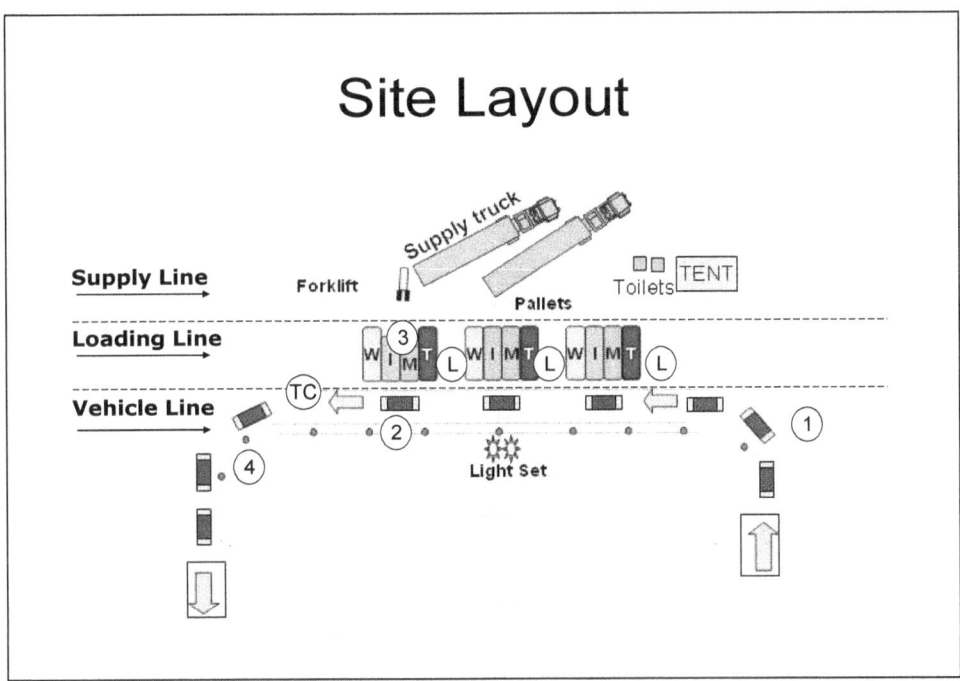

A POD is divided into three areas.

> The **SUPPLY LINE** is where supply trucks, usually tractor-trailers, have room to unload. This area also includes staff care facilities including restroom facilities and rest tent. Having an informational bulletin board in the rest tent is a good way to keep your staff updated.

> The **LOADING LINE** is where supplies are kept waiting on stacked pallets to be distributed to the public. This is also where loaders wait while vehicles are moving through the Vehicle Line.

> The **VEHICLE LINE** is where the public drives through to get supplies. Entry into the vehicle line occurs only when all vehicles have come to a complete stop and the Traffic Controller has instructed the staff to "LOAD".

PODs provide the same quantity of supplies to each vehicle. In the site layout diagram, the POD is providing water (**W**), ice (**I**), shelf stable meals (**M**), and tarps (**T**).

POD

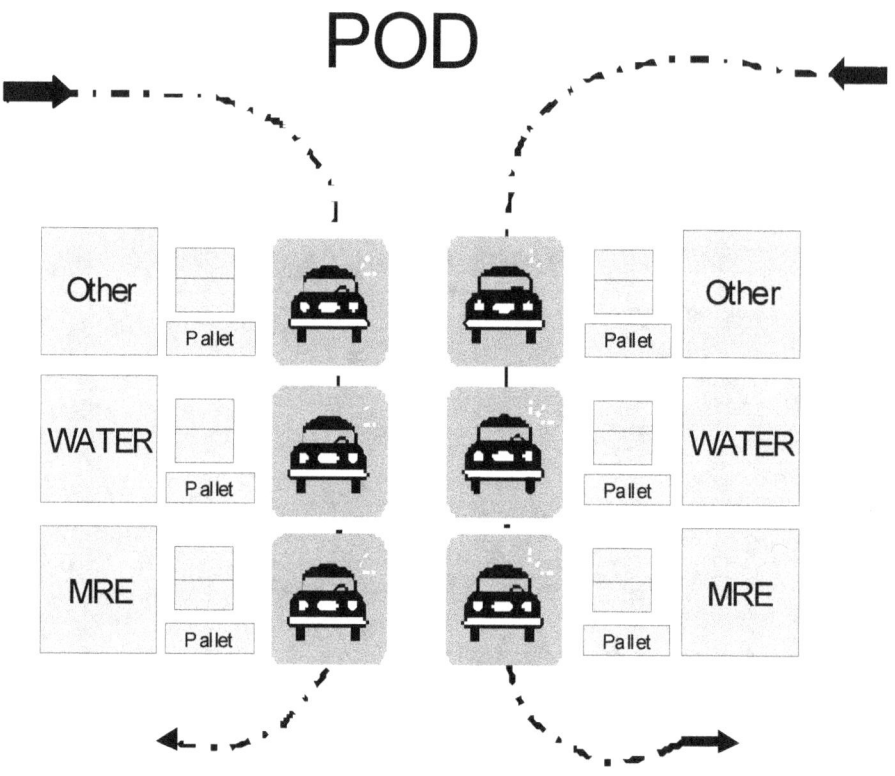

When setting up your POD, there is a minimum space for each area:

- Vehicle Line – 20 feet wide
- Loading Point – 80 feet by 40 feet each
- Supply Line – 50 feet wide

Traffic cones are used to guide customers through the POD site. The standards for placing traffic cones are different for pedestrian and vehicle PODs.

> **For vehicles,** cones should create a lane that is 12 feet wide. It is recommended that cones not be placed more than 20 feet apart.

> **For pedestrians,** cones should create a lane that is 5 feet wide. Cones should not be placed more than 10 feet apart.

Signage for a POD is the same for vehicles and pedestrians.

- **POD Ahead** – this sign provides directions to inbound customers in locating the entrance to the POD. There can be multiple signs placed away from the POD to give the estimated distance to the POD.

- **Enter** – this sign directs customers to enter at the correct point of the vehicle lane.

- **Loading Point** – each loading point should be marked so that customers know to stop for materials to be loaded.

- **Exit/Do Not Enter** – this marks the vehicle lane exit. It is also important to clearly mark the opposite side of the sign with "DO NOT ENTER".

- There are **other signs** you can use at a POD.

    - "This site staffed by..."
    - One Way
    - Turn Here

Loading Points

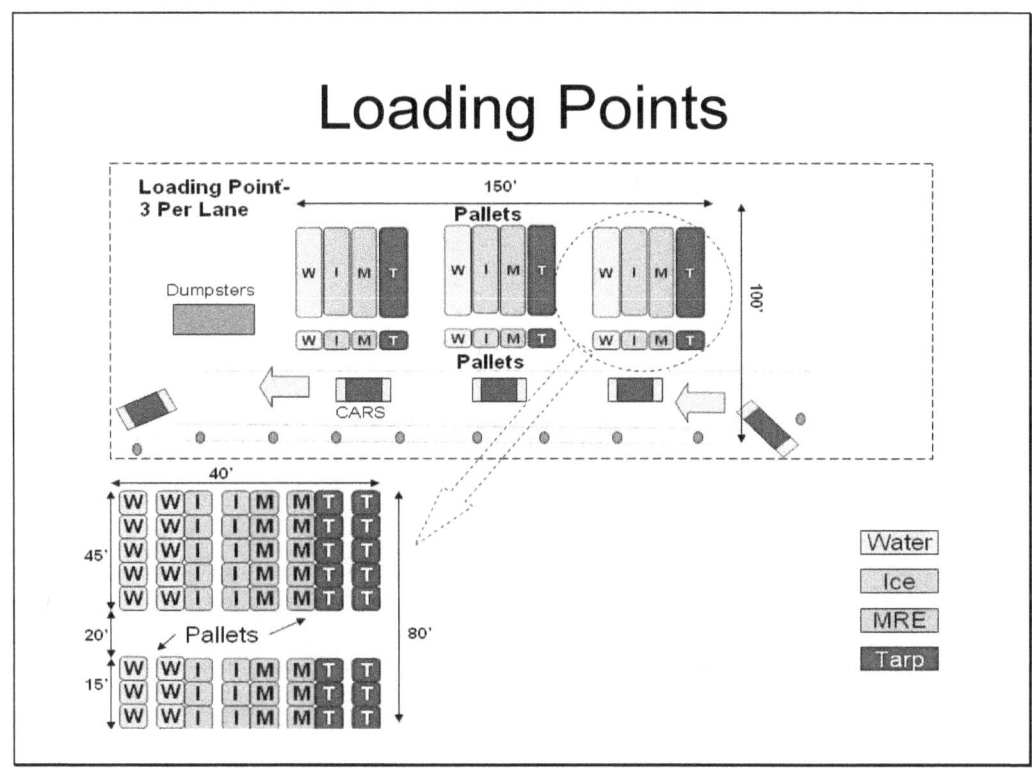

A proper layout of the loading points can ensure a smooth and efficient flow of goods through the POD. Each loading point should be 80 feet by 40 feet. These dimensions are a guide to be adjusted according to the size and quantity of commodities being distributed. In the Loading Points visual, Water (W), Ice (I), MREs (M) and Tarps (T) are being distributed. If the POD is only providing water and food, the loading point could be smaller.

Pallets of commodities must be separated at each loading point. This allows for a more efficient loading and resupply of materials. By mixing pallets of commodities, loaders have to spend additional time sorting.

The United States Army Corps of Engineers has developed a typing standard for PODS. These types are Tier II resource typing definitions and, although accepted throughout most of the nation, are not yet nationally recognized.

The smallest of the PODs is a Type III. A Type III POD serves 5,000 people a day based on one vehicle representing a household of 3 people. A Type III POD is 150 feet by 300 feet and requires a staff of 19 per day and 4 per night.

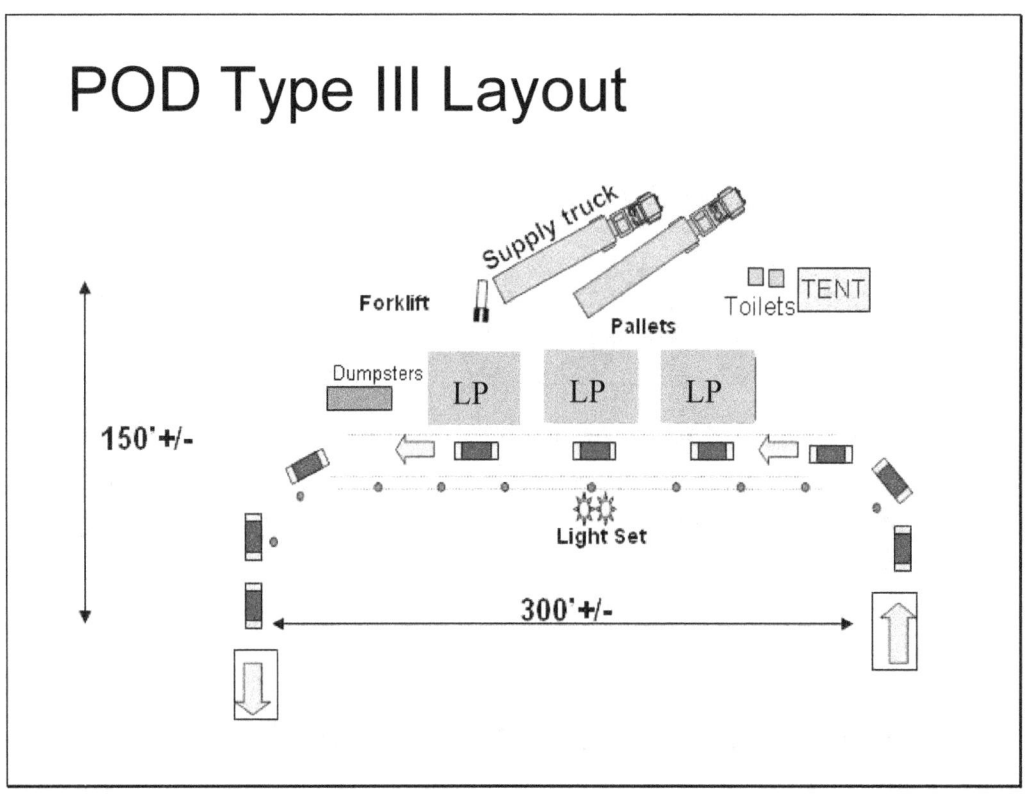

A Type III POD has three loading points and only one vehicle lane.

A Type II POD is twice the size of a Type III and serves 10,000 people a day based on one vehicle representing a household of 3 people. A Type II POD is 250 feet by 300 feet and requires a staff of 34 per day and 6 per night.

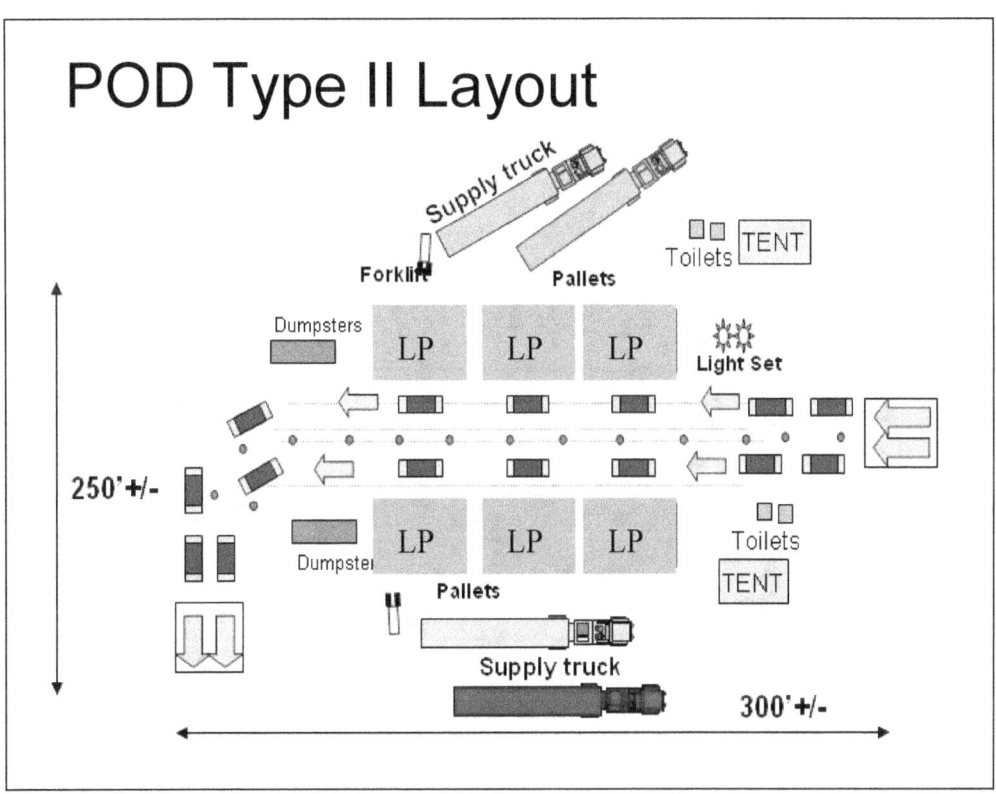

Type II POD has six loading points and two vehicle lanes.

The largest of the PODs is a Type I. A Type I POD serves 20,000 people a day based on one vehicle representing a household of 3 people. A Type I POD is 250 feet by 500 feet and requires a staff of 78 per day and 10 per night. Type I PODs are only used in large metropolitan areas.

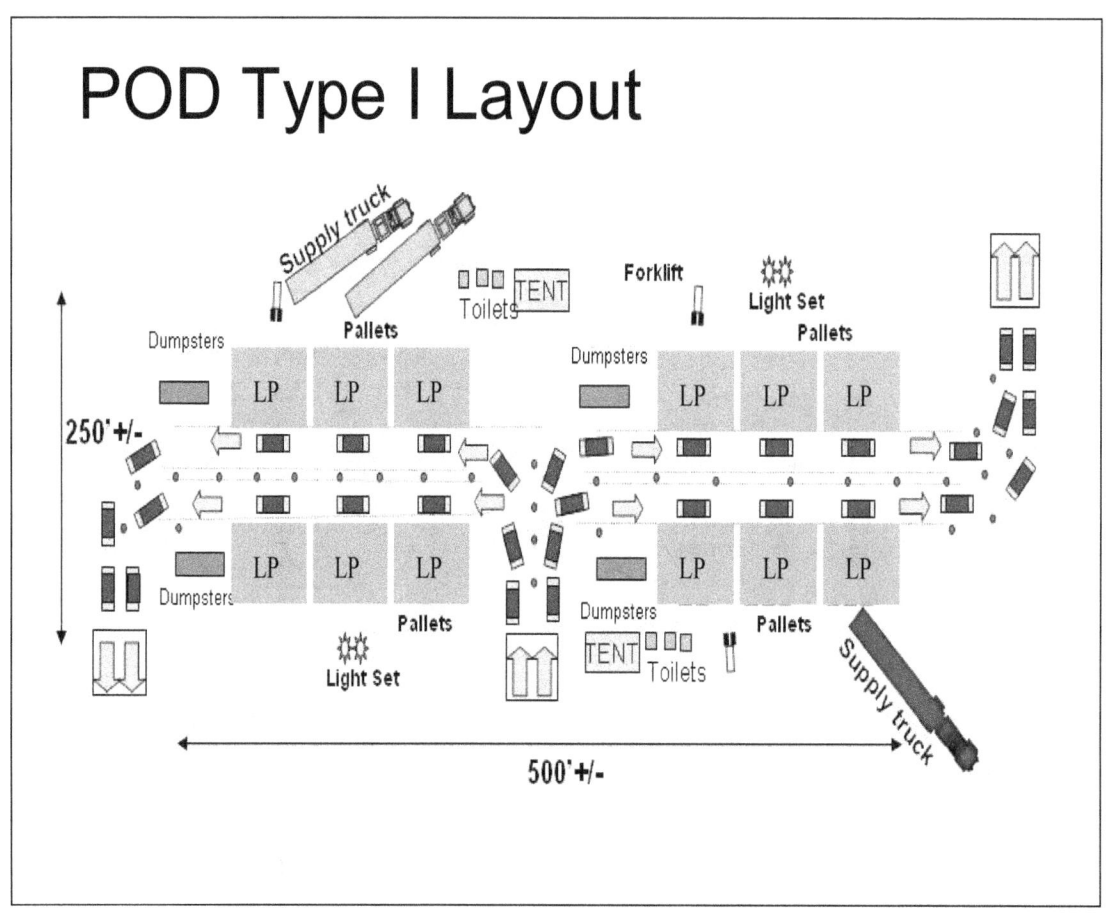

A Type I POD has twelve loading points and four vehicle lanes.

How to Activate a POD

The activation of a POD begins with the notification process. Once an incident occurs, LEMA determines if there is a need for a POD. If needed, LEMA determines the location, timeframe for operation, and what commodities will be provided to the public at the POD. During this time, POD staff should be taking care of their families and homes in preparation for activation.

Once the decision to activate a POD has been made, LEMA contacts the POD manager via phone, radio or messenger and provides, at a minimum, the following information:

- Location of the POD

- Size of POD (Type I, II or III)

- Time and Date POD will open

- Type and quantity of commodities

- Estimated date and time of first supply shipment

The following form can be used to assist in notifying people.

POD ACTIVATION NOTIFICATION FORM		
Line 1	Date and Time of Message	
Line 2	POD Manager Name/Org	
Line 3	Location of POD	
Line 4	Size (by type)	
Line 5	Date to Open	
Line 6	Time to Open	
Line 7	Quantity of Water per Vehicle	
Line 8	Quantity of Food per Vehicle	
Line 9	Type and Quantity of other commodity	
Line 10	Date and Time of First Supply	
Line 11	LEMA Point of Contact	
Line 12	LEMA POC Number	

Note: Line numbers are used for radio communications.

Once the POD Manager is notified, s/he must notify the POD team. This notification could be through a phone tree or by messenger. The team must determine how they will contact each other to activate the POD. As part of the notification, the POD Manager will determine what time the team will assemble at the POD site.

Once the team assembles at the POD site, the POD Manager must conduct a hazard assessment. There may be new hazards on the site in the wake of a disaster. The POD Manager decides if the site is safe for operations. If the site is deemed unsafe, the POD Manager will contact LEMA and report the findings of the hazard assessment. LEMA will determine the next steps.

If the site is deemed safe, the team will begin to set-up the POD. The manager can use the following form to assist in the setup process.

POD Site Setup Checklist

POD Manager: _____

Location: _____

		Yes	No	Remarks
1	Team members arrived			
2	Site hazard assessment complete			
3	Communications established with LEMA			
4	Inspect POD Kit			
5	Determine the location of the Supply, Loading, and Vehicle lines			
6	Establish the port-a-potty location			
7	Establish the dumpster location			
8	Establish the break area location			
9	Set up traffic cones around the vehicle line			
10	Ensure supply trucks can enter and exit			
11	Assign staffing positions			
12	Distribute PPE			
13	Conduct a safety briefing			
14	Determine signage locations			
15	Receive port-a-potties			
16	Receive dumpster			
17	Receive pallet jack			
18	Receive first supply			
19	Notify LEMA that the POD is ready for opening			
20	Put up signage			
21	Open POD			
22	Notify LEMA that the POD is open			

Other Remarks:

POD Manager Initials: _____

Date and Time Complete:

The POD Manager assigns positions based on who is available and who is trained** for specific positions.

The order for filling staff positions is:

- Team Leaders (Support & Loading)
- Traffic Controller
- Community Relations
- Pallet Jack Operator
- Loaders (one per loading point)
- Security Officer
- Additional Loaders

**For new staff and spontaneous volunteers, you may have to provide some Just-in-Time training.

By the time you receive your first supply shipment, you should have at least one pallet jack on site for handling the movement of pallets. When receiving supplies, it is important to track the material that comes in. This is discussed in further detail in the Resource Accountability Lesson.

After direction from LEMA on the POD Type, you will know how many loading points to establish. When setting up a loading point, follow the guidelines provided at the beginning of this lesson.

Once you have your first supply, coordinate with your LEMA to determine when to open the POD to the public. *No earlier than 30 minutes before opening*, place your signage out. This will reduce traffic in the area and set a reasonable expectation with the public. When the site opens, contact LEMA to confirm operations.

How to support a POD site and staff

At each POD location, it is best to have POD kit(s) on site to support the initial setup of the POD. Each POD kit is designed for a Type III POD. If a Type II POD is established at that site, the site should have two kits. A Type I POD would need four kits. The POD kit has supplies for the site and individual staff positions.

POD Kit

One (1) 96 gal trash can, wheeled (for storage of the kit)

Sixteen (16) pairs of leather work gloves

Four (4) rolls of duct tape

Nineteen (19) battery-powered (D-cell) flashlights

Nineteen (19) reflective safety vests

One (1) First Aid Kit

Twelve (12) 36", reflective traffic cones

Sixteen (16) safety hard hats

Thirty (30) orange or red glow sticks

Thirty six (36) D-cell, batteries

Eight (8) medium back support belts or vests

Eight (8) large back support belts or vests

One (1) 5 lb. fire extinguisher

In addition to the resources available in the POD Kit, the site will need, at a minimum, a dumpster, portable restroom, break area, and light set. These will provide support for the staff and allow safer working condition

Summary

In this lesson you learned about:

- Site layout

- POD activation

- Support of POD site and staff

Lesson 4

SETUP

Lesson Objectives

By the end of this lesson you will be able to:

- Describe the equipment you will need at your POD Site

Pallets
Pallet Jack
Fork Lift
Light Tower

This diagram lists the parts of a pallet. Notice where the wheel opening is for the tines of a pallet jack or forklift.

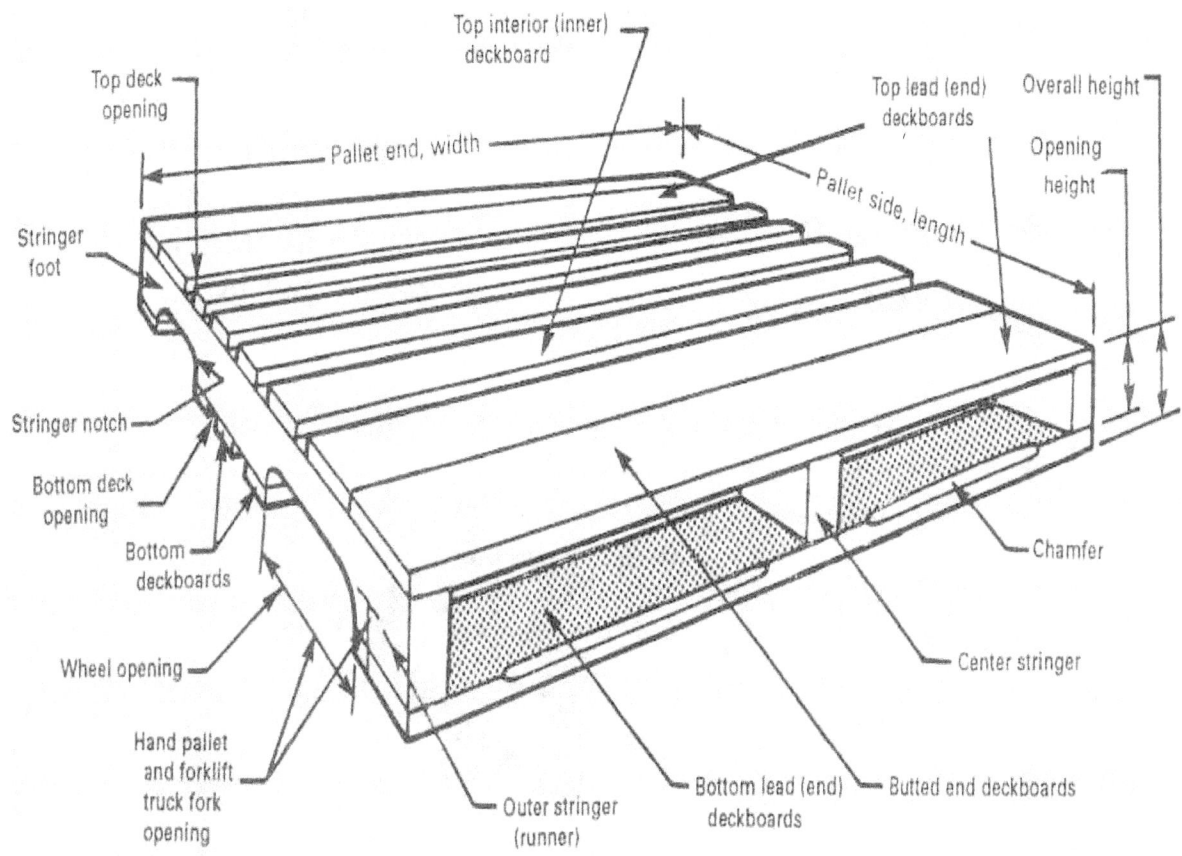

Top interior (inner) deckboard

Top deck opening

Top lead (end) deckboards

Overall height

Pallet end, width

Opening height

Pallet side, length

Stringer foot

Stringer notch

Bottom deck opening

Bottom deckboards

Chamfer

Wheel opening

Center stringer

Hand pallet and forklift truck fork opening

Outer stringer (runner)

Bottom lead (end) deckboards

Butted end deckboards

Pallet Jack

The main parts of a pallet jack are the forks, handle, and actuating lever.

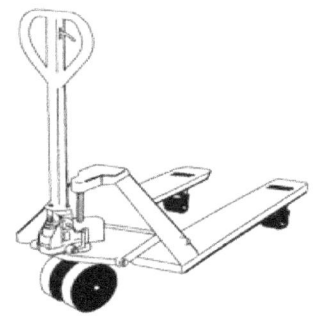

Before inserting the pallet jack into the pallet, ensure that the forks are in their lowest position.

Pallet Jack Handle and Actuating Level

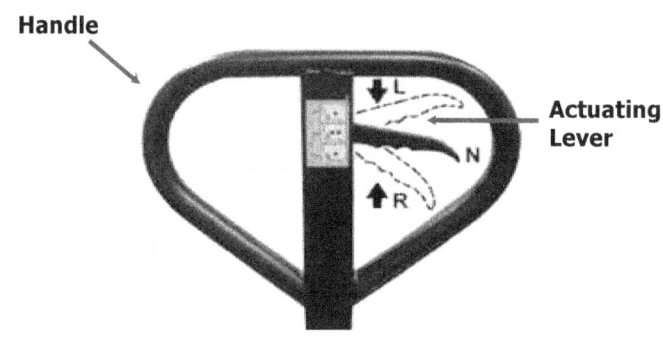

Raise the forks by pushing the actuating lever down (R position on diagram) and pumping the handle up and down. One inch clearance between the floor and pallet is usually sufficient.

Put the actuating lever in a neutral or middle position (N position on diagram) to move the load. This position disengages the lifting mechanism and frees the handle from hydraulic resistance, but keeps the forks raised. When the lever is released, it will automatically return to the neutral position.

Lower the forks by pulling the actuating lever up (L position on diagram) and holding it there until the forks come to a resting position.

Some of the hazards associated with pallet jacks include:

- Load balancing

- Pushing the pallet jack versus pulling

- Controlling the speed of the pallet jack without the assistance of breaks

- Tripping hazard associated with the forks and handle

To mitigate these hazards, follow the following safety rules:

- Always wear provided protective equipment
- Stay out of the vehicle lane when vehicles are moving
- Be alert to your surroundings
- Avoid moving loads up or down ramps
- Do not carry riders
- Center the forks evenly under the load to maintain good balance
- Avoid overloading
- Ensure the stability of the load
- Use both forks for lifting a load
- Pull rather than push loads for increased maneuverability
- Maneuvering loads using the neutral position reduces operator fatigue
- Operate at a controllable speed, since hand pallet trucks do not have brakes
- Park the pallet truck out of traffic areas in a safe, level place with the forks lowered
- The handle should be left in the up position to eliminate tripping hazards

Forklift

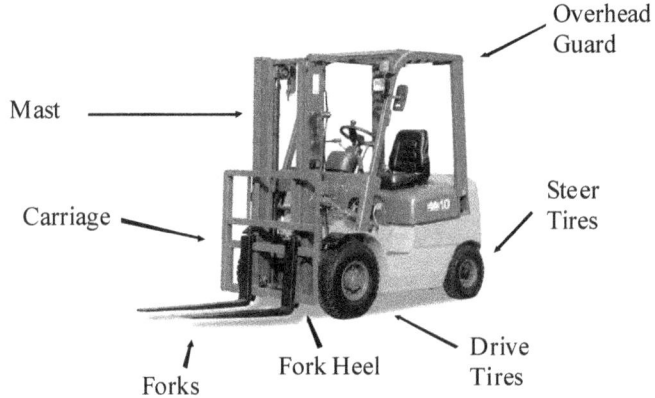

Overhead Guard

Mast

Carriage

Steer Tires

Forks   Fork Heel   Drive Tires

The main parts of a forklift are:

- Mast
- Carriage
- Forks
- Drive Tires
- Steer Tires
- Overhead Guard

When parking a forklift, it is important to follow these steps for safety:

1. Park forklift on flat level surface.
2. Tilt mast to vertical position.
3. Lower forks to floor.
4. Shut engine off.
5. Lock drive wheels.

Forklift Parking

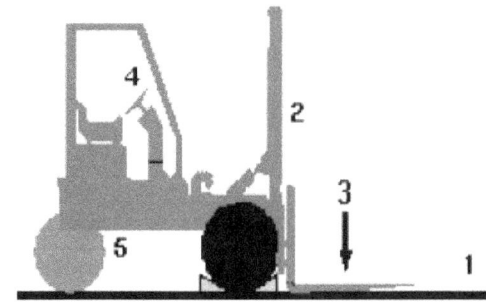

Some of the hazards associated with forklifts include:

- Decreased visibility especially when carrying a load

- Lift height

- Stability on uneven (not level) surfaces

- Steering and turning radius when loaded

- Working around pedestrians

To mitigate these hazards, follow the following safety rules:

> Only authorized and trained personnel (with current certification) will operate the forklift
> Seatbelt must be worn by the operator at all times
> Always wear provided protective equipment
> Stay out of the vehicle lane when vehicles are moving
> Be alert to your surroundings
> Loads will be tilted back and carried no more than 6 inches from the ground.
> Loads that restrict the operator's vision will be transported backwards.
> Forklifts will travel no faster than 5 mph or no faster than a normal walk
> Operator will sound horn and use extreme caution when meeting pedestrians, making turns and cornering
> Operator will assure load does not exceed rated weight limits
> Grades will be ascended or descended slowly. When ascending or descending grades in excess of 10 percent, loaded trucks will be driven with the load upgrade. On all grades the load and load engaging means will be tilted back if applicable, and raised only as far as necessary to clear the road surface
> Do not carry riders
> Center the forks evenly under the load to maintain good balance
> Avoid overloading
> Ensure the stability of the load
> Use both forks for lifting a load
> Pull rather than push loads for increased maneuverability
> Maneuvering loads using the neutral position reduces operator fatigue
> Operate at a controllable speed, since hand pallet trucks do not have brakes
> When un-attended, forklifts will be turned off, forks lowered to the ground and parking brake applied.

Light Tower

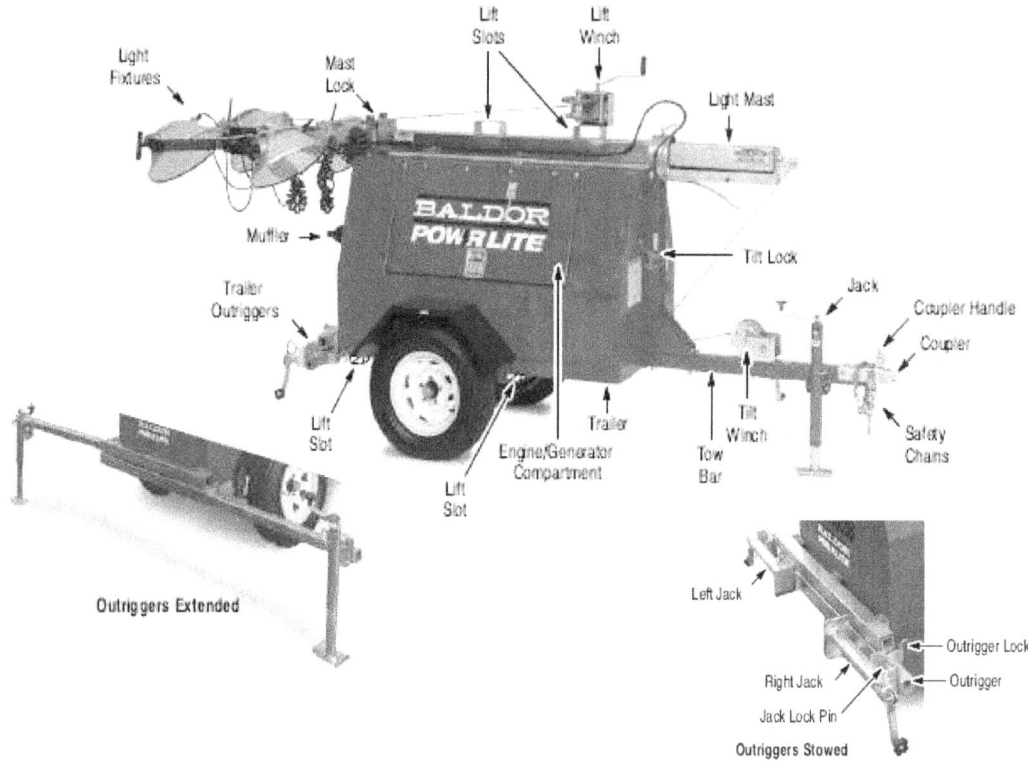

A light tower is used to provide portable lighting and power to the POD site. There are six major systems on a light tower:

- Trailer
- Engine/Generator
- Trailer Stabilization System
- Light Mast
- Light Fixtures
- Electrical System

To set up the light tower:

1. Locate a suitable, level location. Ensure there are no overhead wires or obstructions.
2. Apply and check the parking brake (if equipped).
3. Disconnect the safety chains and trailer light connector from the tow vehicle.
4. Pull the pin on the Front Jack and rotate the jack 90 degrees to the vertical position.
5. Mover the Coupler Handle to the vertical position to release the ball hitch.
6. Use the jack to raise the trailer Coupler from the ball hitch of the tow vehicle.
7. Move the tow vehicle away from the light tower.
8. Pull the Outrigger Lock for the right jack and fully extend the right outrigger. Lock the outrigger into position using the Outrigger Lock.
9. Pull the Jack Lock Pin for the right jack and rotate the jack to the vertical position. Lock the jack in its vertical position using the Jack Lock Pin.
10. Follow steps 8 and 9 for the left outrigger and jack.
11. Adjust the three jacks to level the trailer.
12. With the Light Mast in its stowed position, install or reposition the light fixtures to the desired placement when the tower is raised.
13. Pull the Mask Lock pin so the mast is no longer secured in the stowed position.
14. Pull the Tilt Lock pin so it is not in the way when the mast is raised.
15. Use the Tilt Winch to raise the mast to the vertical position.
16. Secure the mast in the vertical position by inserting and locking the Tilt Lock pin.
17. Use the Lift Winch to raise the mast to the desired height.
18. To rotate the lights, loosen the Mast Rotation Lock, rotate the mast, and tighten the Mast Rotation Lock.
19. Start the generator with the lights off.
20. Once the generator is running at operating speed, turn on each light, one at a time.
21. To stow the light tower, follow the same instructions in reverse.

Summary

In this lesson you learned about:

- Pallets
- Pallet jacks
- Fork Lifts
- Light Towers

Lesson 5

OPERATIONS

Lesson Objectives

By the end of this lesson you will be able to:

- Describe the general operating conditions
- Explain the vehicle line operations
- Explain the loading line resupply operations
- Describe the ordering process
- Understand how to conduct equipment maintenance
- Understand how to work with spontaneous volunteers
- Understand how to handle media and public relations

PODs are generally open to the public for 12 hours a day. This reduces the amount of time the POD is open in low-light conditions.

LEMA will coordinate resupply during the 12 hours the POD is closed. The POD will work with LEMA to determine the hours of operation, but it is recommended that the open hours be from 7am to 7pm and resupply from 7pm to 7am.

The POD Manager will determine breaks for staff including meal breaks. Due to the physical nature of the work, it is recommended that staff get a ten minute break every hour and a twenty minute meal break. Ideally, food will be provided by LEMA at least twice a day (noon and midnight). However, if the situation does not allow delivery of hot food, POD staff are permitted to utilize the shelf-stable meals and water on site for meal breaks.

As already discussed, a POD is divided into three areas:

The **SUPPLY LINE**
The **LOADING LINE**
The **VEHICLE LINE**

POD Operation:

- A vehicle enters the POD
- The Traffic Controller (TC) stands at the front of the vehicle line where all vehicles in the lane can see him/her.
- When the front vehicle is adjacent to the front loading station, the Traffic Controller signals the vehicle to stop. Each vehicle behind the 1st vehicle stops as well.

- Once all vehicles come to a stop, the Traffic Controller blows one long whistle blast and says, with a projected voice, "LOAD". "LOAD" is echoed by the loaders.
- The Loaders (**L**) then load a set amount of supplies from the pallets into the trunk of the vehicle.
- Once the Loaders complete loading supplies into the vehicle, they step back to the loading line and speak with a projected voice "CLEAR"
- When the Traffic Controller hears "CLEAR", s/he visually verifies that all staff and loaders have cleared the vehicle line and, using hand signals, instructs the vehicles to depart the POD and blows a long whistle blast.
- The next set of vehicles enters the vehicle lane and the process repeats.

Consumption Rates

Consumption Rates are determined by the number of customers through a POD per day. This information must be passed on to LEMA each day. This helps to determine POD needs and quantity of supplies to provide.

Ordering

When providing your consumption rates to LEMA, you should also order any supplies you need on the site. Supplies could include fuel for equipment or expendable POD equipment (gloves, vests, etc).

Off Loading Supply Trucks

Resupply should be conducted during the night. The night crew must assist with unloading any supply trucks and organizing the supply and loading lines with the new resources. Commodities should be organized on a first-in/first-out basis.

Resupplying Loading Points

Loading points should be restocked during the night from the supply delivery. During the day, empty pallets should be cleared from the loading line and stored in the supply line for pick-up the following night. It is also advisable to replace empty pallets with full pallets close to the vehicle line to reduce loaders walking excessively to and from the vehicle line.

Maintaining Equipment

Daily Maintenance

On-site equipment must be checked daily to ensure proper working order. The forklift (if on site) should be inspected following the checklist. A similar inspection must be conducted on the pallet jack(s), light tower(s) and other equipment on site.

Break Downs

If, during your inspection or during use, the equipment breaks down, contact LEMA to get a maintenance technician or replacement equipment.

Refueling

Generators and Light Towers should be refueled twice a day prior to shift change. Ensure you follow the owner's manual for proper refueling procedures.

Volunteers, Media, and the Public

Volunteers

At your POD site, you may get volunteers willing to assist you. These volunteers may be from your organization, friends of your staff, or spontaneous public volunteers. You must coordinate the decision to accept volunteers with your LEMA. If the decision is to allow additional volunteers on the POD site, they must follow the same rules and procedures as the trained staff. This includes signing in just as the regular staff does each day.

Media

The media may wish to visit your POD site. This must be coordinated with your LEMA's Public Information Officer (PIO). *All questions from the media must be directed to that PIO.* This ensures a common message across the jurisdiction and other PODs. Your Community Relations staff and POD Manager will be the primary points of contact for media inquiries. Additionally, the media must be directed to not interfere with ongoing POD operations, such as stopping or disrupting traffic flowing in and out of the POD site.

Public Relations

Your Community Relations staff will also provide information to POD customers. This information is provided by LEMA's PIO. The information may be verbal or through handout flyers. The POD Manager should work closely with the Community Relations staff to ensure correct messages are being provided.

Summary

In this lesson you learned about:

- Vehicle line operations
- Loading line resupply
- Ordering
- Equipment Maintenance
- Volunteers
- Media and Public Relations

RESOURCE ACCOUNTABILITY

Lesson Objectives

By the end of this lesson you will be able to:

- Understand the need for accounting for all POD resources
- Track equipment on the site
- Understand the need and process for vehicle counts
- Receive and account for supplies
- Report on current supply inventory
- Report on POD staffing
- Understand how to handle media and public relations

How do you know what equipment is on the site? How will you account for the supplies coming into the POD and being issued to the public? How will you keep track of your staff?

The need for time and resource accounting

Accounting for all personnel, equipment, and supplies at your POD is one of the manager's primary responsibilities. Accuracy in this effort helps ensure that staffing levels are adequate to the task, supplies for the public are maintained at needed levels, and equipment on the site is returned to its point of origin. Additionally, the reports and forms will be used by LEMA to recoup costs once the disaster winds down.

Put together three files for this purpose:

- Equipment
- Resources
- Staffing

Keep an equipment inventory

Your POD could have equipment from several different sources – two forklifts from two different rental agencies, a POD kit from LEMA, a borrowed pallet jack from a local business. Keeping track allows you to know what you should have on hand for use and provides an easy reference tool to get them back to their point of origin when closing the POD.

Defective or missing equipment should be reported. You may request a replacement, although in a major disaster replacements may not be immediately available.

Sample Equipment Inventory Form

- Keep complete list of equipment on site
- Provides a quick reference when closing the POD and returning equipment

POD Equipment Inventory					
Date	Types of Equipment	Serial Number	Condition	Owner Name (Company, Jurisdiction)	Location
	POD Kit				

This form can serve as the basis for your equipment file. Be sure and keep copies of any equipment transfer forms and inventories (such as the POD Kit inventory) in your file as back up to this form to provide additional detailed information.

- ➢ Enter the date you received the equipment
- ➢ What kind of equipment
- ➢ Serial number (if any)
- ➢ The condition of the equipment (i.e., "complete" for kits, "leaking hydraulics", "dented front right fender", "no defects", etc.)
- ➢ Where it came from
- ➢ Its location in the POD (supply line, loading line, etc.)

Vehicle Counts help establish actual consumption rates

Vehicle counts are important for a number of reasons. By gathering basic statistics on the number of customers served, you can gain an understanding of what will be needed to continue to provide goods at each POD. In addition, it helps the POD manager track the actual amount of goods issued so s/he can report on this.

To that end, there should be a **Check-in Specialist** position. This person should keep a running tally on a clipboard as vehicles arrive at the check in point and provide the information to the POD manager upon request.

Receiving supplies

As supplies arrive at the POD, the manager should use the trucker's Bill of Lading or Mission Assignment Form to account for the supplies being delivered. If there is a discrepancy, the manager should contact the point of origination (the staging area or vendor) and discuss the difference. If a resolution of the discrepancy cannot be reached, the manager should make a note of the discrepancy (and steps taken) on the form before signing. Do not sign the form without including this information. In any case, the manager should never accept supplies without signing for them.

Daily inventory reporting

Daily reporting of inventory to LEMA allows accurate restocking. LEMA will tell you when and how to report each day (they may want a verbal report instead of a written one) and what elements of information it wants. Usually, the basic items to report for each type of supply are:

- quantities received
- quantities distributed
- quantities on hand

Using a supply inventory form will help you keep track.

Sample Supply Inventory Form

- Used for daily inventory tracking
- Provided to local emergency management agency

POD Supply Inventory Form							
Date	Time	Truck #	Mission #	Type of Supply	Qty Rec	Qty Dist	Bal on Hand

This form will provide the basis for your supply file. Be sure to keep Bills of Lading or Mission Forms as back-up to this, or any form that you use. Vehicle counts are also useful documentation in this file.

The supply inventory form is useful for capturing all incoming and outgoing supplies, as well as balancing inventory levels. The form itself may or may not be required by LEMA, but the information you gather will need to be reported.

As inventory is received, enter the date, time, truck number, mission number from the trucker's mission form, the type of supply (water, MRE, etc.), the quantity received, and the new balance on hand at the POD. For supplies being issued, make entries at regular intervals during the operational period. A suggestion is to do this hourly, but you decide when this will be for your POD. For these entries, record the date, the time, the type of supply, the amount distributed and the balance on hand. You may decide to use a form for each type of supply or use one form for all types. This form is useful because it allows you to keep track of your supplies on a regular basis and keep better control of your inventory.

Another suggestion is to use a summary form for daily reports. This example of a POD Daily Report form is provided for that purpose. Enter only the balances on this form and use your inventory form as detailed back up.

POD DAILY REPORT		
Line 1	Date of Message	
Line 2	Time of Message	
Line 3	Manager Last Name	
Line 4	Managing Organization	
Line 5	Location	
Line 6	Date Opened	
Line 7	Quantity of Water Received (gal)	
Line 8	Quantity of Water Distributed (gal)	
Line 9	Quantity of Food Received (each)	
Line 10	Quantity of Food Distributed (each)	
Line 11	Quantity and Type of Other Commodity Received	
Line 12	Quantity and Type of Other Commodity Distributed	
Line 13	Number of Day Staff	
Line 14	Number of Night Staff	
Line 15	Number of Unassigned Staff	
Line 16	Number of Spontaneous Volunteers	
Line 17	Initials of Reporting Manager	

Staff reporting to LEMA

Daily reporting of staffing to LEMA helps them keep a handle on POD activities and your staffing needs.

At a minimum, you should be prepared to include the number of people assigned to the day shift and night shift. If you have unassigned personnel, they may be able to use them at another location. The reverse is also true – another site may have extra people and you need them. Additionally, it is very important that spontaneous volunteers are reported to LEMA.

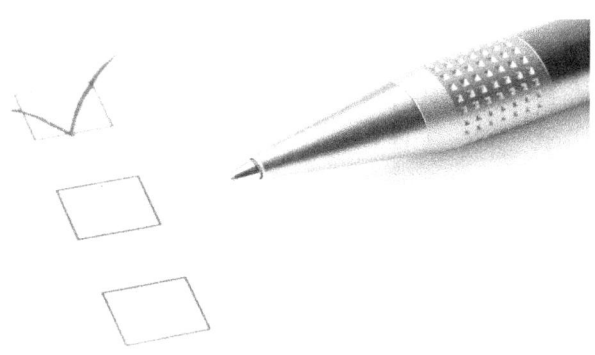

Basic elements of personnel report are:

- Assigned personnel
- Unassigned personnel, and
- Spontaneous volunteers

As with inventory reporting, LEMA will tell you when and how to report each day, and what elements of information are needed. The Daily Activity Report is a part of emergency worker management and is a good way to gather the reporting information you need.

This form (courtesy of Washington State) can be found at http://emd.wa.gov under Search and Rescue.

Sample Staff Reporting Form

- **Daily Activity Report**
  - Form # EMD-78
  - Found under Search and Rescue at http://emd.wa.gov
  - Use to document emergency workers
  - Provide to LEMA

STATE OF WASHINGTON
EMERGENCY WORKER DAILY ACTIVITY REPORT

County in which mission/incident took place: _____

Mission/Incident Number: _____

Mission/Incident Name: _____ Date From: _____ Date To: _____

Unit Name: _____
Unit Address: _____

EMERGENCY WORKER NAME	CARD No.	ASSIGNMENT OR TEAM	DATE		DATE		DATE		TOTAL HOURS	ROUND TRIP MILES (DRIVER)
			IN	*OUT	IN	*OUT	IN	*OUT		
1.										
2.										
3.										
4.										
5.										
6.										
7.										
8.										
9.										
10.										
11.										
12.										
13.										
14.										
15.										
16.										
17.										
18.										
19.										
20.										
21.										
22.										
23.										
24.										
25.										
26.										
27.										
28.										
29.										
30.										

* The time a person could reasonably have expected to reach home without stopping enroute.

TOTAL PERSONNEL: _____ TOTAL HOURS: _____ TOTAL MILEAGE: _____

THIS FORM MUST BE SIGNED BY LOCAL EMERGENCY MANAGEMENT DIRECTOR/COORDINATOR OR SHERIFF'S DEPUTY.
By my signature below, I certify that these persons did participate in this mission/incident:

Print Name and Title _____ Signature _____

EMD - 078 (02/00)

Keep a form like this Daily Activity Report in your staff file. It is useful for capturing data on staffing levels and activities. A new form should be completed each day (including the day shift and night shift). Enter the incident information at the top as soon as you get the form. The mission number and incident name will be provided by LEMA. The unit name and address is the name and location of your POD.

Each member of your team, including yourself, should be entered.
- Name
- Worker number or Drivers License number
- Which position you assigned them to
- Time began working and time they stopped followed by total hours worked

There are multiple columns for time began and stopped for when individuals need to leave for a period of time. The round trip mileage column is to record total mileage of those who have to commute and/or are sent on a mission during their shift.

It is extremely important that you record all personnel working on this form as it becomes a part of the official record for the disaster. It is especially important to record spontaneous volunteers as this form is their proof that they worked the disaster.

The form is ultimately needed by LEMA, but they may ask you to do your daily report verbally or written in summary form and collect more detailed forms later. As with inventory reporting, the daily reporting form below can be useful for summary reporting.

POD DAILY REPORT		
Line 1	Date of Message	
Line 2	Time of Message	
Line 3	Manager Last Name	
Line 4	Managing Organization	
Line 5	Location	
Line 6	Date Opened	
Line 7	Quantity of Water Received (gal)	
Line 8	Quantity of Water Distributed (gal)	
Line 9	Quantity of Food Received (each)	
Line 10	Quantity of Food Distributed (each)	
Line 11	Quantity and Type of Other Commodity Received	
Line 12	Quantity and Type of Other Commodity Distributed	
Line 13	Number of Day Staff	
Line 14	Number of Night Staff	
Line 15	Number of Unassigned Staff	
Line 16	Number of Spontaneous Volunteers	
Line 17	Initials of Reporting Manager	

Summary

In this lesson you learned about:

- Time and Resource Accounting
- Equipment Inventories
- Vehicle Counts
- The process for receiving incoming supplies
- Reporting processes and forms

Lesson 7

SAFETY

Lesson Objectives

By the end of this lesson you will be able to talk about:
- Overall safety
- POD Manager Role in Safety
- PPE
- Lifting
- Fire Extinguishers
- Weather Injuries
- Hazard Communication
- Workplace Violence

It is important to understand the difference between a hazard and a risk. A hazard is an inherent property or source of danger such as "height". A risk is the extent to which a hazard such as "height" can cause harm. For example, what are the chances of falling? Risks from hazards can be reduced or removed by taking safety precautions. However, you cannot remove the underlying hazard itself.

Overall Safety Practices

- Inspect work area daily
- Be an observer—stay alert--THINK
- Housekeeping
- Ask questions
- Report inquiries/incidents/illnesses
- Report safety issues to your supervisor

It's been said many times before, but it's still true: *Good safety practices include everyone on the worksite.* All workers should inspect their work area daily and be aware of changing hazards. Always be alert to your surroundings and stop any unsafe act you observe.

- One way to be safe is to keep your assigned work area clean and clear of hazards.

- The best defense to hazards is to think! Think through your actions before you do them.

- If you have a question regarding safety, do not hesitate to ask a co-worker or supervisor.

- If an injury, incident, or illness occurs on the worksite, report it to your supervisor and fill out the proper paperwork. It is important for your safety and the safety of others to report any safety issues you observe to your supervisor.

The POD Manager's role in site safety

The POD Manager is the primary safety officer and is responsible for the safety of all staff and visitors to the site. The POD Manager trains the staff on proper and safe operation of all equipment and ensures safety measures are enforced. The POD Manager conducts safety training with staff and provides a safety briefing at the beginning of each shift. The POD Manager accomplishes a site hazard assessment daily, develops preventive safety measures and communicates this to all staff. *Most importantly, the POD Manager sets the example for the rest of the staff in his/her actions.* This encourages positive behavior from the staff and assists in the enforcement of safety rules.

The POD Manager conducts acident investigations and develops preventive measures based on the outcome of the investigation. Additionally, the POD Manager should be open to the observations of his/her staff. A daily safety briefing must be presented to all POD staff at the start of each shift. The safety brief should contain, at a minimum, the following information:

- Review of the Daily Site Hazard Assessment Form
- Reminder to use and care for PPE
- Prevention of weather related injuries
- Changes to the HAZMAT on site
- Any additional safety items for discussion

DAILY SITE HAZARD ASSESSMENT FORM			
Inspected by: _____	Date: _____		
Location: _____	Time: _____		

Training:	Yes	No	Comments
Is each person assigned to a job within their capability?	☐	☐	
Did each person receive a safety brief at shift change?	☐	☐	
Is training on PPE and equipment provided?	☐	☐	
Environment:	Yes	No	Comments
Are resources available to deal with very hot or very cold conditions? (drinking water, heated tent, shade)	☐	☐	
Does staff know the symptoms of heat cramps, heat stroke, hypothermia?	☐	☐	
Is the level of light adequate for safe and comfortable performance of work?	☐	☐	
Housekeeping:	Yes	No	Comments
Is the work area clear of debris and tripping hazards?	☐	☐	
Are materials properly stacked and spaced?	☐	☐	
Are work areas clear of fluid spills or leakage?	☐	☐	
Are aisles and passageways clear of obstructions?	☐	☐	
Are walkways clear of holes, loose debris, protruding nails, and loose boards?	☐	☐	
Is the break area kept clean and sanitary?	☐	☐	
Are the dumpsters being serviced properly?	☐	☐	
Are the restrooms (portable or fixed) clean, sanitary and restocked?	☐	☐	
Personal Protective Equipment:	Yes	No	Comments
Is required equipment provided, maintained and used?	☐	☐	
Does equipment meet requirements?	☐	☐	
Are warning signs prominently displayed in all hazard areas?	☐	☐	
Material Handling and Storage:	Yes	No	Comments
Is there safe clearance for all equipment through aisles and doors?	☐	☐	
Is stored material stable and secure?	☐	☐	
Are storage areas free from tipping hazards?	☐	☐	
Are only trained operators allowed to operate forklifts?	☐	☐	
Do personnel use proper lifting techniques?	☐	☐	
Vehicle Traffic:	Yes	No	Comments
Are cones placed to direct traffic?	☐	☐	
Is the vehicle line free of pedestrians when vehicles are moving?	☐	☐	
Are pedestrian and vehicular traffic separated?	☐	☐	
ADDITIONAL COMMENTS OR CONCERNS			

Be sure to inform LEMA of any accidents *immediately.* Any accidents could result in claims. Early notification will help identify if there is a process problem that may occur in other PODs and needs to be fixed.

When an injury or incident occurs on the POD site, an accident investigation must be conducted by the POD Manager. This investigation aids in recognizing workplace hazards and reducing further risk by implementing mitigating efforts. These reports allow the POD Manager to identify trends in accidents and assists with the filing of workers' compensation claims. At no time are these reports intended to place blame on an individual or group.

Forms used during an accident and incident investigation include:

ACCIDENT INVESTIGATION REPORT

This form is used as the initial reporting of an accident and will assist in filling out the Supervisor's Report of an Accident. You can print a sample form at:

http://www.lni.wa.gov/WISHA/Rules/corerules/Help fulTools/HT12-CR.doc

SUPERVISOR'S REPORT OF AN ACCIDENT

This form is the official report of an accident and used for documenting injuries and causes. It can be found at:
http://www.lni.wa.gov/forms/pdf/417048a0.pdf.

WITNESS STATEMENT

This form is supplemental to the Supervisor's Report of an Accident. It is used to record witness statements of the accident. A Witness Statement form can help document the findings of an investigation into an accident or incident in your workplace. You can copy and use this form or make your own. This can be found at:
www.lni.wa.gov/forms/pdf/416093a0.pdf

REPORTING REQUIREMENTS:

A major accident occurs when there is a fatality or an incident causes two or more persons to be taken to the hospital. If a major accident occurs, the POD manager must contact LEMA immediately. The POD Manager will complete an Accident Investigation Report and provide that to LEMA.

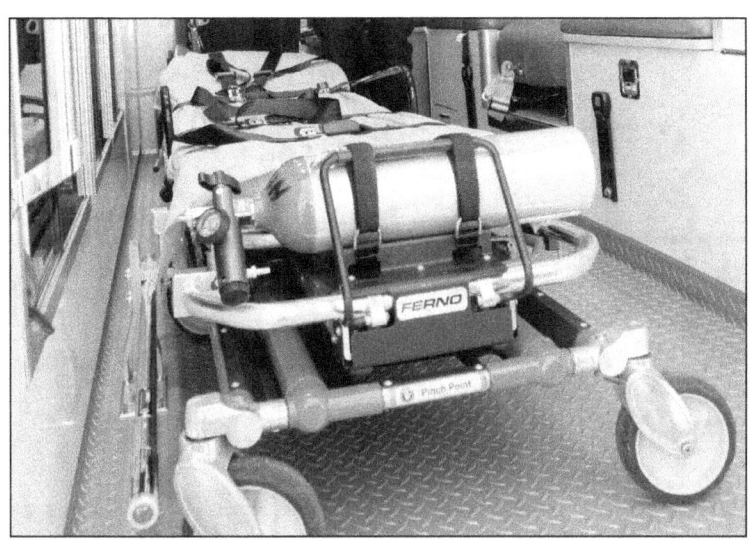

Proper Lifting

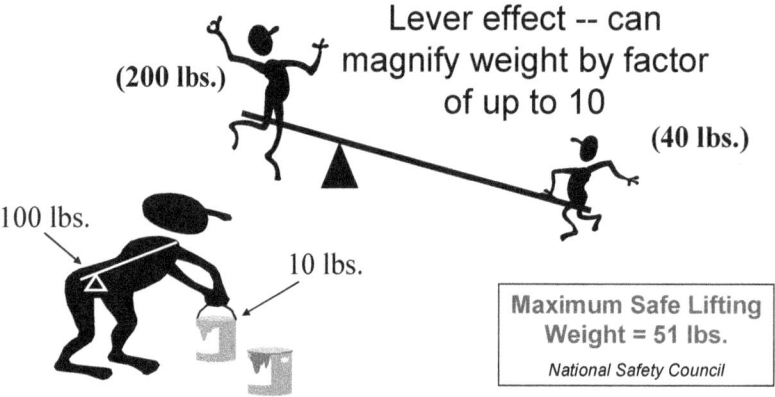

Improper lifting can lead to back, leg and arm pain. Poor techniques can cause both acute injury and serious chronic effects. Proper lifting will help you avoid these problems.

When carrying a load, ensure you carry it close to your body. If not, you will be forcing your body to carry more weight due to the lever effect.

Proper Lifting

Proper lifting is accomplished using a four step process:

1. Plan ahead.

   Before attempting to lift or move something heavy, step back and analyze what needs to be accomplished. How heavy is the object? How far does it have to be moved, and where it is going to end up? What is the shape of the object? Is it cumbersome? Will it be easily manipulated? Is it a two-person job? Is there anything in the way that needs to be moved prior to lifting?

2. Lift close to your body.

   You will be a stronger and more stable lifter if the object is held close to your body rather than at the end of your reach. Make sure you have a firm hold on the object you are lifting, and keep it balanced close to your body.

3. Feet shoulder width apart.

    Stand directly in front of the load with feet about shoulder width apart. One foot should be in front of the other for balance. A solid base of support is important while lifting. Holding your feet too close together will be unstable, too far apart will hinder movement. Keep the feet about shoulder width apart and take short steps.

4. Bend your knees and keep your back straight.

    Bend the knees and tighten the stomach muscles. Using both hands, grasp the object firmly and pull it as close as possible to your body. Since leg muscles are stronger than back muscles, lift with the legs, until they are straightened.

    When it is time to set the load down, it is very important that it is done correctly. Reverse the procedures for lifting to minimize the strain on the back. If the load is going on the floor, bend the knees and position the load in front of you. If the load is to go at table height, put it down and keep in contact with the load until it is secure on the table.

Once you are carrying the load, there are additional safety precautions to take.

- Ensure you can see over the load. Even if you can see over the load, realize that you will have limited visibility.

- Avoid jerky movements and twisting your body. Keep the natural curve in the spine; don't bend at the waist. To turn, move the feet around by pivoting on the toes, not by twisting at the stomach.

- Watch out when passing by another object to ensure you do not pinch your fingers. This is especially true for doorways.

- Always face the direction you are moving. This will keep you more stable.

Quick tips for lifting can be found at
http://www.lni.wa.gov/IPUB/417-055-909.pdf

Fire Extinguisher

 • **Class A** - Wood, paper, cloth, trash

 • **Class B** - Flammable liquids, oil, gas, grease

 • **Class C** - Electrical, energized electrical equipment

• **Class D** - Combustible metals

Fire extinguishers are divided into four categories, based on the types of fires:

Class A extinguishers are for ordinary combustible material such as wood, paper, cloth, trash and most plastics.

Class B extinguishers are for flammable or combustible material including oil, gas and grease.

Class C extinguishers are for electrical fires and the extinguishing agent is non-conductive.

Class D extinguishers are for chemical fires including combustible metals such as magnesium, potassium and sodium.

Fire extinguishers, using different extinguishing elements, are capable of extinguishing combinations of these fire classes:

Water – only in Class A fires

Dry Chemical – Class A, B, & C fires

- Sodium Bicarbonate
- Monoammonium phosphate

Carbon Dioxide – Class B and C fires

To use a fire extinguisher, remember PASS:

P – PULL THE PIN at the top of the extinguisher. The pin releases a locking mechanism and will allow you to discharge the extinguisher

A – AIM at the base of the fire and not at the flames. You must extinguish the fuel to the fire.

S – SQUEEZE the lever. This will release the extinguishing agent in the extinguisher. If the handle is released, the discharge will stop.

S – SWEEP from side to side. Using a sweeping motion, move the fire extinguisher back and forth until the fire is completely out.

Before deciding to fight a fire, be certain that:

- The fire is small and not spreading
- You have the proper fire extinguisher
- The fire will not block your exit (keep the exit at your back)

NEVER FIGHT A FIRE IF:

- The fire is spreading rapidly
- You don't know what is burning
- You don't have the proper fire extinguisher
- There is too much smoke or you are at risk of inhaling smoke

REMEMBER—Operate the extinguisher from a safe distance.

A typical fire extinguisher lasts for about 10 seconds. Once the fire is out, don't walk away. Watch the area for a few minutes in case it re-ignites.

How to prevent weather injuries

Working in hot weather can be dangerous. The hazards of working in hot weather include:

- Sun burn
- Heat exhaustion
- Heat cramps
- Heat stroke
- Heat rash
- Dehydration

To prevent a hot weather injury:

- Drink small amounts of water frequently
- Avoid alcohol and caffeinated drinks
- Wear light-colored, loose-fitting, breathable clothing
- Take frequent short breaks in cool shade
- Keep skin covered
- Use sunscreen with an SPF of at least 30
- Wear a hat with a wide brim
- Wear UV-absorbent sunglasses
- Irrational behavior

Recognize the signs of a hot weather injury:

Sunburn
Chills
Fever
Flu-like symptoms
Heat Stroke
- Confusion
- Irrational behavior
- Loss of consciousness
- Convulsions
- Lack of sweating
- Abnormally high body temperature

Heat Cramps
- Painful muscle spasms
Heat Exhaustion
- Headache
- Nausea
- Dizziness
- Weakness
- Thirst
- Giddiness
Heat Rash
- Red cluster of pimples or small blisters
Dehydration
- Thirst
- Lack of sweating

If you see the signs of a hot weather injury, seek medical attention immediately.

Working in cold weather can be dangerous too. Hazards include:

- Hypothermia
- Frostbite
- Aggravation of medical conditions like arthritis
- Increased risk of musculoskeletal injuries

To prevent a cold weather injury:

- Wear multiple layers of light, loose-fitting clothes
- Limit skin exposure by wearing gloves, hat, and scarf (as much as 40% of your body heat can be lost from an uncovered head)
- Keep hydrated but avoid caffeinated and alcoholic drinks
- Avoid sweating (sweating hinders the insulating value of clothing)
- Do not overexert and overheat yourself

Recognize the signs of a cold weather injury:

- Excessive shivering
- Blue lips and fingers
- Slurred speech
- Poor coordination
- Impaired thinking
- Pain or numbness in extremities

If you see the signs of a cold weather injury, seek medical attention immediately.

Personal Protective Equipment [PPE]

Some of the types of PPE used on a POD site include:

- Head Protection
  - Hard Hats
- Hand Protection
  - Leather Work Gloves
- High Visibility Vests
  - Reflective traffic vests for all personnel
  - Must be worn when on site!
- Illumination
  - Flashlights
  - Glow sticks

Hazard communication

Everyone has the right and responsibility to be aware of all hazards and proper work procedures for hazardous material used in their work area.

Some hazardous material that could be on the POD site includes fuel for generators and vehicles, batteries, glow sticks, and MRE heaters.

Information on the hazards present on a POD site is found on hazardous material labels and material safety data sheets.

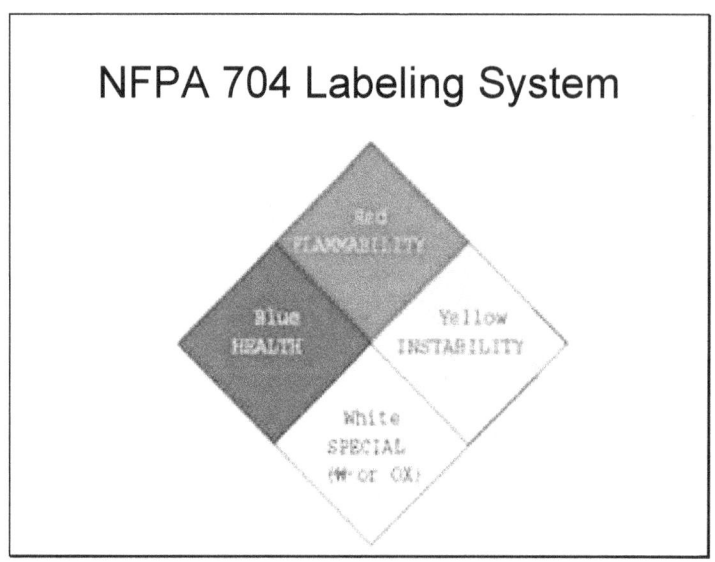

The NFPA 704 is a standard that provides a readily recognized, easily understood system for identifying specific hazards and their severity using spatial, visual, and numerical methods to describe in simple terms the relative hazards of a material. It addresses the health, flammability, instability, and related hazards that may be presented as short-term, acute exposures that are most likely to occur as a result of fire, spill, or similar emergency.

The system is characterized by the "diamond shape" or "square on point." Hazard severity is indicated by a numerical rating from zero (0) indicating a minimal hazard, to four (4) indicating a severe hazard. In addition to spatial orientation, the hazards are also color coded: blue for health hazards, red for flammability, and yellow for instability.

The severity rating for each hazard can be found at:

http://www.nfpa.org/faq.asp?categoryID=928&cookie%5Ftest=1#23057

Other symbols, abbreviations, and words that some organizations use in the white Special Hazards section are shown below. These uses are **not** compliant with NFPA 704, but we present them here in case you see them on an MSDS or container label:

ACID	This indicates that the material is an acid, a corrosive material that has a pH lower than 7.0
ALK	This denotes an alkaline material, also called a base. These caustic materials have a pH greater than 7.0
COR	This denotes a material that is corrosive (it could be either an acid or a base).
	This is another symbol used for corrosive.
	The skull and crossbones is used to denote a poison or highly toxic material. See also: CHIP Danger symbols.
	The international symbol for radioactivity is used to denote radioactive hazards; radioactive materials are extremely hazardous when inhaled.
	Indicates an explosive material. This symbol is somewhat redundant because explosives are easily recognized by their Instability Rating.

http://www.ilpi.com/msds/ref/nfpa.html

A Material Safety Data Sheet or MSDS is prepared by chemical manufacturers or importers to describe characteristics of the product and to provide information concerning potential hazards. They must be readily available for employee review at all times in the workplace. Additionally, all employees must receive training on the MSDS for each hazardous material on site that is used in a commercial manner.

The MSDS information answers these questions:

- What is the material and what do I need to know?
- What hazards are associated with the material?
- What should I do if a hazardous situation occurs with that material?
- How can I prevent hazardous situations from occurring?
- What protective equipment should be used with the material?

Material Safety Data Sheet	
I. Identification of Product	V. Reactivity Data
II. Hazardous Ingredients	VI. Health Hazards
III. Physical and Chemical Characteristics	VII. Precautions for Safe Handling and Use
IV. Fire and Explosion Hazard	VIII. Control Measures

You can find more information about each of these sections by going to

http://www.pp.okstate.edu/ehs/hazcom/Hc-msds.htm

Workplace violence

Even in the most respectful and low stress environments, incidents of workplace violence can and do still occur. In a POD environment, during the aftermath of a major disaster, the stressors on victims and families can be even greater. It is therefore important to understand the stages of workplace violence, indicators of risk, and what to do and not do in the event of workplace violence.

Workplace violence includes verbal threats and assaults in addition to physical assaults. Most workplace violence follows five stages:

> **Confusion** - Behavior characterized by bewilderment or distraction. Unsure or uncertain of the next course of action.

> **Frustration** - Behavior characterized by reaction or resistance to information. Impatience. Feeling a sense of defeat in the attempt of accomplishment. May try to bait you.

> **Blame** - Placing responsibility for problems on everyone else. Accusing or holding you responsible. Finding fault or error with the action of others. They may place blame directly on you. Crossing over to potentially hazardous behavior.

> **Anger** - Characterized by a visible change in body posture and disposition. Actions include pounding fists, pointing fingers, shouting or screaming. This signals very risky behavior.

> **Hostility** - Physical actions or threats which appear imminent. Acts of physical harm or property damage. Out-of-control behavior signals they have crossed over the line.

As a POD worker, you should be aware of behavior that could lead to a workplace violence incident. These indicators include:

- Sudden and persistent complaining about being treated unfairly

- Blaming of others for personal problems

- Sudden change in behavior, deterioration in job performance

- Statement that he or she would like something bad to happen to supervisor or another co-worker

- Paranoid behavior

- Sudden increased absenteeism

- Sexually harassing, or obsessing about a co-worker: sending unwanted gifts, notes, unwanted calling, stalking

- Increased demand of supervisor's time

- Alcohol or drug abuse

- Talking to oneself

- Instability in family relationships

- Financial problems combined with not receiving a raise or promotion

- Poor relationships with co-workers or management

- History of violent behavior

- Previous threats, direct or indirect

- Presenting and talking about reading material that is violent in nature

- Carrying a concealed weapon, or flashing one around

- Quiet seething, sullenness

- Refusal to accept criticism about job performance

- Sudden mood swings, depression

- Sudden refusal to comply with rules or refusal to perform duties

- Inability to control feelings, outbursts of rage, swearing, slamming doors, etc.

When dealing with a frustrated person,

DO:

- Project calmness, move and speak slowly, quietly and confidently

- Be an empathetic listener. Encourage the person to talk and listen patiently

- Focus your attention on the person to let him/her know you are interested in what s/he has to say

- Maintain a relaxed yet attentive posture and position yourself at a right angle rather than directly in front of the other person. Acknowledge the person's feelings. Indicate that you can see s/he is upset.

- Use delaying tactics which will give the person time to calm down. For example, offer a drink of water (in a disposable cup).

- Be reassuring and point out choices. Break big problems into smaller, more manageable problems.

- Accept criticism in a positive way. When a complaint might be true, use "it was my fault." If the criticism seems unwarranted, ask clarifying questions.

- Ask for his/her recommendations. Repeat back to him/her what you feel s/he is requesting of you.

- Arrange yourself so that the person cannot block your access to an exit.

DO NOT

- Reject all of a client's demands from the start.

- Use styles of communication that generate hostility such as apathy, brush off, coldness, condescension, going strictly by the rules, or giving the run-around.

- Pose in challenging stances such as standing directly opposite someone, hands on hips or crossing your arms. Avoid any physical contact, finger pointing or long periods of fixed eye contact. Make sudden movements which can be seen as threatening. Note the tone, volume, and rate of your speech.

- Challenge, threaten, or dare the individual. Never belittle the person or make him/her feel foolish.

- Criticize or act impatiently toward the agitated individual.

- Attempt to bargain with a threatening individual.

- Try to make the situation seem less serious that it is.

- Make false statements or promises you cannot keep.

- Try to impart a lot of technical or complicated information when emotions are high.

- Take sides or agree with distortions.

- Invade the individual's personal space. Make sure there is a space of three feet to six feet between you and the person.

http://www.doli.state.mn.us/pdf/vguideapg.pdf

Summary

In this lesson you learned about:

- General Safety Procedures
- POD Manager Role in Safety
- PPE
- Lifting
- Fire Extinguishers
- Weather injuries
- Hazard Communication
- Workplace Violence

Lesson 8

DEMOBILIZATION

Lesson Objectives

By the end of this lesson you will understand how to:

- Close your Site
- Turn in Excess Supplies
- Return Equipment
- Clean and Replenish the POD Kit
- Submit Paperwork

Closing your Site

The need for a POD is based on a lack of infrastructure (roadways, power, water) to support normal distribution of food, water, or other supplies. Once the local infrastructure starts coming back, close your POD. For example, if your POD is in the parking lot of a grocery store, once the electricity and roadways are back to working order and the store begins receiving stock, you don't want to interfere with their operation. The community can begin to support itself again.

LEMA will let the POD manager know when it is time to close the POD. LEMA has the overall picture of the community and can best judge when recovery has reached a point that the community can sustain itself. LEMA can close all PODs or only those at specific sites.

It is important to remember that even if PODs are closing in nearby locations, yours may need to remain open a bit longer. Infrastructure restoration may be more difficult in some areas than in others.

Turn in Excess Supplies

Once you have received a POD closure notice from LEMA, you will need to block the vehicle or pedestrian lane to further traffic and clear the loading line of any remaining supplies. Ask LEMA for instructions on where to send any remaining customers. Remember to be polite and helpful to people – some of them may still need help.

Consolidate supplies by type (water with water, food with food, etc.) onto pallets in the supply line for loading back onto the truck. Inventory anything remaining prior to loading on the truck. It may be helpful to request a strapping unit or plastic wrap from LEMA to help you secure loose supplies to their pallets before loading them.

Use a blank POD Supply Tracking Form to record remaining inventory balances and provide it to the truck driver as a Bill of Lading. Be sure to keep a copy of the form for your records. Load the supplies on the truck and begin cleaning the supply line.

Once all supplies are loaded and off site, consolidate your equipment behind the supply line and use your equipment inventory form to confirm everything is present.

If equipment is missing, check with your workers to see who had it last and where it was located. You will need to generate a written statement on any missing equipment. Damage can occur to equipment during normal use. Don't worry about these situations – it is expected and will be handled by LEMA. When you contact LEMA for pick up, be sure to report any damaged or missing equipment so they can take any necessary further action.

Once you have accounted for everything, contact LEMA to schedule a pick up of the equipment for return to the owners. If you negotiated for use of a piece of equipment, you may return it to the proper owners yourself.

Clean and Replenish the POD kit

Once your equipment and supplies are cleared, finish cleaning the site and collect the elements of your POD kit for repacking. Use the kit inventory sheet to ensure all elements are returned, inspect them for damage and clean them prior to repacking. Report any damaged or missing items to LEMA for replacement.

It is important to restore the kit as close to original condition as possible to ensure it is ready for the next time it is needed. Repack the kit to its original configuration.

In some cases, the kit was issued by LEMA, in others it may have been stored on site in preparation for use. Regardless, return it to the location from which it was issued.

At this point your site should be completely cleaned up. Remember, some sites will be located on commercial properties. We need to maintain good will with the owners so that we can use their sites again should the need arise.

Final reports are important in two regards.

- Provides you and your staff with a comprehensive look at what you accomplished. Your efforts helped many people weather the disaster and, in some cases, actually saved lives!

- Provides LEMA with documentation they can use to recoup some of their costs related to the disaster.

Take a moment to make some notes on what you saw during POD operation. What went right? What needs improvement? Refer to your Supply Tracking Forms and daily reports to generate a final count of the amount of each supply you distributed (how much water, food, and other supplies were issued) and how many people or vehicles you served.

Once you have your totals calculated, gather your staff for an After Action Review. Report your activity totals to them and congratulate them on their work. Highlight what went right and recognize those who went the extra mile, then discuss anything that you noted for improvement. Ask for their input on both good and bad aspects of the operation. Add their input to your notes. Be sure to send them home knowing that they provided a significant service at a time when they were really needed.

Provide your activity totals and after action notes along with your personnel, equipment, and resources files to LEMA. You should keep a copy of the files for your organization as well so your activities are documented internally and so you have something to refer to should LEMA contact you later for information.

Your POD is now officially closed.

Summary

In this lesson you learned:

- Who authorizes closure of a POD
- The process for returning supplies and equipment
- Repacking and returning the POD kit
- Completing an After Action Review with your staff
- Preparing and submitting final reports to LEMA

Lesson 9

ADOPT-A-POD PROGRAM

Lesson Objectives

By the end of this lesson you will be able to:

- Define the Adopt-a-POD program

- Delineate responsibilities for the program

- Make an informed decision about implementing this in your jurisdiction.

What is the Adopt-a-POD Program?

The "Adopt-A-POD program" is a program for recruiting volunteers to staff Points of Distribution in your community where they will distribute life sustaining emergency commodities to the public following a disaster or emergency.

Who can Adopt-a POD?

Any Community Based Organization, Volunteer Service Organization, Faith Based Organization, or private business that has an Adopt-A-POD Agreement with a local jurisdiction. For example, a school, a civic organization, a church group, or a private industry could agree to serve the community by "adopting" a POD site. Individuals are also encouraged to volunteer.

What does the Program do?

 The Adopt-a-POD Program *does*:

- Provide guidance (training should be provided locally).

- Support and emphasize partnerships between public governmental agencies and the private sector to include volunteer agencies, non-governmental agencies (NGO), community based organizations (CBO), faith based organizations and businesses.

- Maintain focus on all hazards disaster planning and management including terrorism.

- Require implementation and activation by local jurisdictions.

- Supplement current processes and procedures.

 The Adopt-a-POD Program *does not*:

- Guarantee POD locations and staff.

- Guarantee resources for POD operations or the resources provided to the public (food, water, etc).

- Replace any already existing or future programs or processes at the state or local jurisdiction.

Roles and Responsibilities

State

State Emergency Management Division
- Assign a Program Administrator
- Program Administrator
  - Establish and maintain standard procedures and implementing instructions to provide a uniform, statewide implementation of the Adopt-A-POD Program
  - Provide, maintain and update all forms and training material for the Adopt-A-POD Program
  - Provide materials, information packets, signs, logos, and any other items or materials used to implement and promote the Statewide Adopt-A-POD Program
  - Contact each participating jurisdiction a minimum of once a year to monitor the program.
  - Provide safety information and training aids to the participating jurisdictions for training of participating organizations.
  - Furnish a POD kit for each identified POD location.

Local Jurisdiction

- Abide by all terms and conditions of any POD Intergovernmental Agreement.
- Maintain the Adopt-A-POD Program at the local level.
- Recruit participating organizations.
- Ensure all participating organizations abide by the terms and conditions of the agreement.
- Identify POD staffs and register them as necessary. Background checks are at the discretion of the local jurisdiction.
- Provide representative(s) to attend POD Manager Training.
- Provide training for POD Managers.

Participating Organization

- Provide a designated POD Manager.
- Abide by all terms and conditions of any agreement.
- Provide training to all identified POD staff.
- Conduct a functional or full scale exercise of the POD a minimum of once a year.
- Ensure the safety of all POD staff and customers.
- Maintain and store the organization's assigned POD kit.

POD Manager

- Attend the POD Manager Training provided by the State EMD or local jurisdiction.
- Provide training for all participants using the safety information and training aids provided by the Program Administrator and local jurisdiction.
- Ensure all POD Staff is properly accounted for during training, exercises and actual activations.

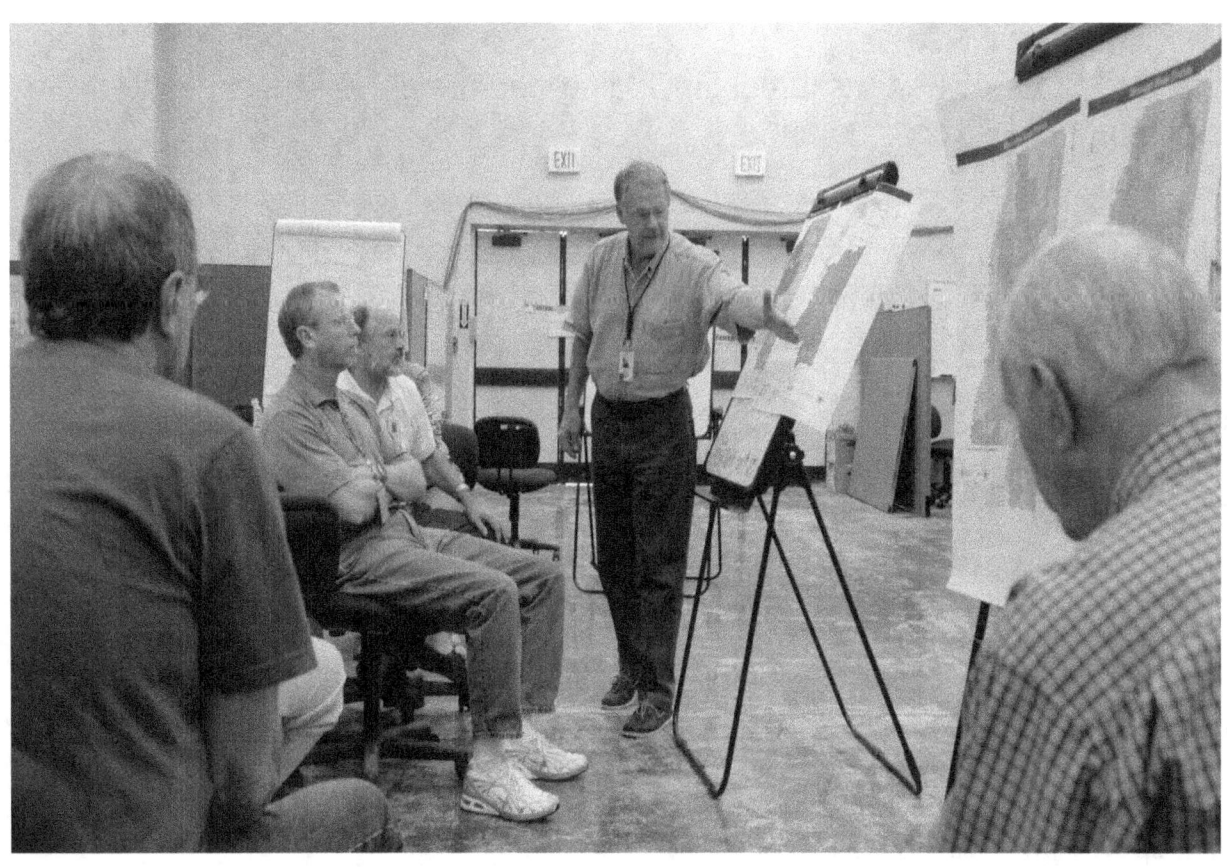

Some emergencies or disasters will occur with enough warning that appropriate notification will be issued to ensure some level of preparation. Other situations will occur with no advanced warning.

A Catastrophic Event or series of concurrent smaller events will require a vast amount of emergency resources in order to respond to the emergency needs of affected communities.

Citizens, businesses, state agencies, and industries will provide their own resources for the first three days; however, the need may exist to provide a limited amount of life sustaining resources to the community due to loss of infrastructure.

Local jurisdictions will comply with any and all administrative codes regarding the program and operation of PODs.

Local and State owned resources, including personnel, will be exhausted quickly in a catastrophic event.

Points of Distribution will be needed at the local level to support the distribution of life sustaining supplies to the community.

Military (Department of Defense, Reserve Forces, National Guard, and State Militia) resources may not be available to support operations due to other national security missions.

Local jurisdictions may not have the personnel available to staff Points of Distribution due to other emergency response roles and responsibilities.

Citizens and businesses will be interested in supporting their communities by participating in this program.

Participation from jurisdictions

Any city, county, or tribal jurisdiction within the state may participate in the Adopt-a-POD program. To apply for participation, it is suggested that a jurisdiction provide a State POD Agreement Form. An example **POD Organizational Agreement** from the Washington State Emergency Management Division is included in this lesson.

The jurisdiction should identify the number of PODs by type and identify possible locations for PODs or at least identify the general areas of coverage needed. This information will help focus the jurisdiction to areas that require coverage.

Identify organizations to participate in the program.
- Promoting Sponsorship. Jurisdictions are encouraged to promote the Adopt-A-POD Program to identify potential participating organizations. This public outreach can include:
    1. Letters to organizations
    2. Newspaper Article
    3. Community group meetings
- Sign-up. Upon identification of a participating organization, the following must be completed:
    1. POD Agreement signed. A copy of the form is kept with the local jurisdiction.
    2. POD Staff completes all necessary paperwork as defined by the state or local jurisdiction.
    3. POD Kit is delivered, inventoried, and signed for.
    4. One or two "POD Managers" are identified. These POD Managers should attend POD Training within three months of the agreement (as available).
- POD Manager Training. Jurisdictions will provide POD Manager Training.
- Bi-Annual Update. Upon completion of the two year obligation, if a participating organization wishes to renew their agreement, the local jurisdiction has the option of renewing the agreement. A new agreement will be signed and kept on file. If the participating organization does not wish to renew the agreement, the POD Kit will be returned to the jurisdiction.

- Recognition. Jurisdictions are encouraged to recognize participating organizations for their commitment to assist their communities. Examples of possible forms of recognition include:
  1. Certificate of Appreciation for the Organization
  2. Plaque
  3. Recognition in a jurisdiction newsletter
  4. Letter of Appreciation signed by the senior executive officer
- Jurisdictions may utilize the volunteer time towards cost sharing during an actual event in accordance with 44 CFR Chapter 1.

Participation from organizations

Organizations that wish to adopt a POD should contact their local emergency management agency. The Organization can provide staff or staff and a location for the POD. The local emergency management agency makes the determination if the location fits the requirements as a POD and meets the intent of the jurisdiction's POD forecast model.

Upon notification that the POD site is suitable, the participating organization will identify a POD Manager, sign the Adopt-A-POD agreement, and pick up their POD Kit.

Organizations will adopt a POD for a period of no less then two years. The POD Manager is required to attend the POD Manager Training within three months of signing the agreement. The Organization is required to conduct a POD exercise a minimum of once a year. The Organization must provide the exercise date(s) to the local emergency management agency a minimum of 30 days prior to the exercise.

POD Organizational Agreement

Draft Example provided courtesy of Washington State's

Adopt-a-POD Program

Jurisdiction Symbol	Group Name and Address:
Agreement Number:	

THIS AGREEMENT is made and entered into by and between [City, County, Tribe], hereinafter called the "Jurisdiction" and the above named group, hereinafter called the "Group."

WHEREAS, the Jurisdiction is a participant of the Washington State Emergency Management Division's Adopt-A-POD Program, and whereas, the Group wishes to contribute toward the effort to support the community during and after an emergency or disaster;

NOW THEREFORE, the Jurisdiction does hereby grant the Group permission to participate in the Adopt-A-POD Program by establishing and staffing a Community Point of Distribution (POD) as authorized by the Jurisdiction, in accordance with the following terms and conditions:

The Group does hereby agree to adopt _____ Community Point of Distribution for a period of not less than two years and agrees:

1. To conduct activities in a safe manner and comply with any conditions as may be required by the Jurisdiction for safety of participants. Safety is the number one priority of the program.

2. To assign a POD Manager to represent the Group and coordinate the activities at the assigned Community Point of Distribution. The POD Manager shall have a copy of this Agreement and copies of all Washington State Emergency Worker forms with him/her while the Community Point of Distribution is active. The POD Manager will attend POD Training provided by the Jurisdiction.

3. To store the assigned POD Kit assigned to the Community Point of Distribution and inventory the kit once a quarter.

4. To have all participants wear the safety equipment furnished by the Jurisdiction when participating in the Community Point of Distribution activities.

5. Participants shall be 16 years of age or older. The Group shall furnish supervision by one or more adults for every eight minors (under 18 years of age) participating in the activity.

6. Each participant shall, before participating in the Community Point of Distribution activities, attend a training and safety brief provided by the POD Manager or the Jurisdiction.

7. To comply with the Adopt-A-POD program specifications when participating in an active Community Point of Distribution.

8. To not possess or consume alcoholic beverages while at an activated Community Point of Distribution.

9. To conduct training and exercises on operating a Community Point of Distribution a minimum of once a year. Notification of training and exercises must be annotated on an EMD-079 Training Request Form and submitted to the local Emergency Management Agency a minimum of 30 days prior to training.

10. To provide the local Emergency Management Agency a copy of the completed EMD-078 Form with names and time worked of individual participants in the authorized activity within 7 calendar days following each training, exercise, and actual activation.

11. That the POD Manager shall report any injuries incurred by participants during maintenance activities to the local Emergency Management Agency within two working days of the injury. Notification should include Name of Injured Person, Nature of Injury, Date and Time of Injury, How the Injury Occurred.

12. To return all assigned POD Kit supplies to the Local Emergency Agency at the termination of this agreement.

The Jurisdiction does hereby agree to:

1. Provide a complete POD Kit, safety materials, and training to the POD Manager.

2. Maintain necessary records required under RCW 38.52 to secure medical aid benefits for participants.

Other Considerations, Terms and Conditions:

It is recommended the Group have at least one person with a valid First Aid/CPR card be present during activities.

It is also recommended the Group have a cellular phone, radio, or some form of two-way communications on site to coordinate with the local Emergency Management Agency and in case of emergency.

The Jurisdiction is authorized to terminate this Agreement without notice if it deems it necessary, for any reason, or if the Group fails to comply with any conditions of this Agreement or the Adopt-A-POD program specifications, or for any public purpose, without cost to the Jurisdiction. This Agreement will automatically terminate upon 30 days written notice of non-compliance, unless the Group takes corrective action(s).

The term of this Agreement shall commence on _____ , and shall end on _____ unless renewed, or terminated on 30-day notice by the Jurisdiction, or the Group.

The Group and its agents agree to protect the state of Washington and the Jurisdiction, its officers and employees and save them harmless from all claims, actions or damages of every kind and description which may accrue to or be suffered by any person, persons, or property by reason of the acts or omissions of the Group or its agents in use or occupancy of the airport right of way or in the exercise of this Agreement.

In case any suit or action is brought against the State of Washington or the Jurisdiction, its officers and/or employees, arising out of or by reason of any of the above causes, the Group and its agents will, upon notice of such action, defend the same at their sole cost and expense and satisfy any judgment against the State of Washington or the Jurisdiction, its officers, or employees: PROVIDED, that if the claims or damages are caused by or result from the concurrent negligence of (a) State of Washington's agents or employees, (b) the Jurisdiction's agents or employees and (c) the Group or its agents, this indemnity provision shall be valid and enforceable only to the extent of the negligence of the Group or its agents.

The Group and on behalf of its assigns and agents agrees to waive any claims for losses, injury to persons and or property, expenses, damages or lost revenues incurred by it or its agents in connection with Group, its assigns or agents in the use or occupancy of the airport right of way or in the exercise of this Agreement against the State of Washington, the Jurisdiction, its agents or employees except the reasonable costs of repair of property resulting from the negligent injury or damage to the Group's property by the State of Washington, the Jurisdiction, its agents, or employees.

Group

By: _____
Representative

Title: _____

Date: _____

Jurisdiction

By: _____
Representative

Title: _____

Date: _____

Summary

In this lesson you learned:

- About the Adopt-a-POD program

- Roles and Responsibilities in the program

- What to consider when planning your program

CONCLUSION

Lesson Objectives

By the end of this lesson you will be able to identify:

- What you learned from this Guide

- Next steps in setting up the POD program in your state

- Ways in which your state's POD program can improve

What did you learn?

Answer the following questions to help identify your key learning points.

1. The three most important things I learned from this guide are:

2. Now that I have read this guide and watched the DVD, my next steps as a POD Manager or Local Emergency Manager are:

3. I think PODs would run smoothly in my community if we could:

Point of Distribution – A location established by a local jurisdiction to provide life sustaining commodities (food, water, etc) to the public in the aftermath of an emergency or disaster when the surrounding infrastructure is incapable of sustaining demand

Fire Hazard – or Flammability. The ability of a material to ignite and burn readily.

Hazard Communication – information and training on the proper handling and use of hazardous material.

Health Hazard – a chemical for which there is statistically significant evidence that acute or chronic health effects may occur in exposed employees.

Heat Cramps – painful muscle spasms resulting from an electrolyte imbalance normally caused by the lack of water replenishment.

Heat Exhaustion – a mild form of heat stroke.

Heat Rash – An inflammatory skin condition caused by obstruction of the ducts of the sweat glands, resulting from exposure to high heat and humidity and characterized by the eruption of small red papules accompanied by an itching or prickling sensation

Heat Stroke – the most serious heat related disorder and occurs when the body's temperature regulation fails and the body temperature rises to critical levels.

Local Emergency Management Agency – An organization with the authority to perform local emergency management functions.

Local Jurisdiction – Any City, Town, County or Tribe.

Material Safety Data Sheet – document that contains information on the potential health effects of exposure to chemicals, or other potentially dangerous substance, and on safe working procedures users should adhere to when handling chemical products.

Participating Organization – Any community based organization, faith based organization or private business that signs an agreement with a local emergency management agency to adopt a Point of Distribution.

Personal Protective Equipment – all clothing and other work accessories designed to create a barrier against workplace hazards.

POD Manager – person identified by the participating organization that manages the operation of a Point of Distribution.

Public Information – Providing information to the public including, but not limited to, current situation, safety precautions, emergency contact information, and emergency instructions or guidance.

Shelf Stable Food – Food that does not require heating, cooling, or special equipment to open and eat (for example, MREs).

Workplace Violence – assaults, other violent acts or threats which occur in or are related to the workplace and entail substantial risk of physical or emotional harm to individuals, or damage to government resources or capabilities.

Acronyms

ACID – Acid

ALK – Alkaline

COR – Corrosive

POD – Community Point of Distribution

DOSH – Division of Safety and Health (formally WISHA)

HAZMAT – Hazardous Material

I – Ice

LEMA – Local Emergency Management Agency

LP – Loading point

M – Shelf stable meals

MRE – Meals, Ready to Eat

MSDS – Material Safety Data Sheet

NFPA – National Fire Protection Agency

OSHA – Occupational Health and Safety Administration

PASS – Pull, Aim, Squeeze, Sweep

PIO – Public Information Officer

POD – Point of Distribution

PPE – Personal Protective Equipment

SPF – Sun Protection Factor

T – Tarps

USACE – United States Army Corps of Engineers

W – Water

W̶ – Use no water

WAC – Washington Administrative Code

Websites

Accident Investigation Report

http://www.lni.wa.gov/WISHA/Rules/corerules/HelpfulTools/HT12-CR.doc

Material Safety Data

http://www.pp.okstate.edu/ehs/hazcom/Hc-msds.htm

Quick tips for lifting

http://www.lni.wa.gov/IPUB/417-055-909.pdf

Severity ratings for specific hazards

http://www.nfpa.org/faq.asp?categoryID=928&cookie%5Ftest=1#23057

Special Hazards

http://www.ilpi.com/msds/ref/nfpa.html

Staff Reporting Form

http://emd.wa.gov

Supervisor's Report of an Accident

http://www.lni.wa.gov/forms/pdf/417048a0.pdf

Witness Statement

www.lni.wa.gov/forms/pdf/416093a0.pdf

Workplace violence

http://www.doli.state.mn.us/pdf/vguideapg.pdf

Special Thanks

State of Washington

State of Texas

United States Army Corps of Engineers—Readiness Center

Federal Emergency Management Agency—Emergency Management Institute

———◆———

To access the on-line exam and receive a certificate for course completion please:

1. Go to **http://training.fema.gov**
2. Click "FEMA Independent Study" on the top menu bar
3. Select "ISP Course List"
4. Scroll to and click on "IS-26 Guide to Points of Distribution (PODS)"
5. The final exam can be found on the right.

———◆———

To order additional guides please call

FEMA Publication Warehouse
1-800-480-2520